Washed and Waiting

Reflections on Christian Faithfulness and Homosexuality

By

Wesley Hill

16

EasyRead Large

RHYW

Copyright Page from the Original Book

We want to hear from you. Please send your comments about this book to us in care of zreview@zondervan.com. Thank you.

ZONDERVAN

Washed and Waiting
Copyright © 2010 by Wesley Hill

This title is also available as a Zondervan ebook. Visit www.zondervan.com/ebooks.

This title is also available in a Zondervan audio edition. Visit www.zondervan.fm.

Requests for information should be addressed to:

Zondervan, Grand Rapids, Michigan 49530

Library of Congress Cataloging-in-Publication Data

Hill, Wesley, 1981-
    Washed and waiting : reflections on Christian faithfulness and homosexuality / Wesley Hill.
        p. cm.
    ISBN 978-0-310-33003-5 (softcover, gatefold)
    1. Homosexuality—Religious aspects—Christianity. 2. Gays—Religious life. 3. Hill, Wesley, 1981- I. Title.
    BR115.H6H55 2010
    248.8'408664—dc22
                                                 2010005802

Cover design: Rob Monacelli
Cover photography: Tomek Sikora
Interior design: Matthew VanZomeren

Printed in the United States of America

---

10 11 12 13 14 15 /DCI/ 19 18 17 16 15 14 13 12 11 10 9 8 7 6 5 4 3 2 1

ReadHowYouWant partners with publishers to provide books for ALL Kinds of Readers. For more information about Becoming A (RHYW) Registered Reader and to find more titles in your preferred format, visit:
www.readhowyouwant.com

TABLE OF CONTENTS

Praise for Washed and Waiting

Wesley Hill's work is a combination of profound personal honesty and deep pastoral reflection. His academically gifted mind applied to the careful exegesis of God's Word has led him to countercultural yet biblical conclusions and applications. Wesley's passion to glorify Jesus by living faithfully as a Christian man who happens to have a homosexual orientation is an inspiration to every struggling believer who wishes things were different than they are. His insights and biblical reflections will be a substantial help to many fellow agonizers as they live out their faith in a fallen world. This book can provide life-changing encouragement to any believer who yearns to be faithful to the God who has accomplished salvation—a salvation that is already but not yet. For we who are in Christ are all "washed and waiting."

Tom Steller, academic dean, Bethlehem College and Seminary

Wesley Hill has written a courageous book. His story will resonate with the unique experience of other Christians with same-sex feelings they did not choose. But his theological perspective broadens his message to include all believers who are struggling to live faithfully in a broken world. This book will also challenge churches to be communities of costly love where men and women can be real with each other.

Mardi Keyes, L'Abri Fellowship

Washed and Waiting is vividly written and deeply reflective. It is also an enormously risky project in that it openly presents Wesley Hill's struggles to come to terms with his sexuality and his hard-won decision to live a celibate life. Books on this subject may be intelligent *or* theologically responsible *or* honest, but I've never seen one that possessed all three virtues—until now. Any Christian who wants to grapple seriously, biblically, and charitably with human sexuality must read this book.

Alan Jacobs, Clyde S. Kilby professor of English, Wheaton College

Like a well-crafted tapestry, *Washed and Waiting* skillfully weaves biblical commentary with personal reflection as it leads the reader inside a Christian life lived amidst the reality of homosexuality. Gently iconoclastic and courageously human in its authenticity and transparency, Wesley Hill instructs and humbles both head and heart as he unpacks the pain, confusion, deep sense of loss, and loneliness of the faithful Christian homosexual person's walk. There is, however, no hand-wringing here. Few books have left me with as much hope as *Washed and Waiting.*

Christopher W. Mitchell, Marion E. Wade

professor of Christian Thought, Wheaton College

This is an incredibly important book that moves beyond the usual faceless arguments and Christian rhetoric and instead is someone's actual story—a story that tells of someone who has maintained the truths of Scripture and fleshes them out in real life. It is a raw, insightful, honest, beautiful, gut-wrenching, gripping story that I pray many people will read. I thank Wesley Hill for the courage to share this message in a culture that desperately needs to hear it.

Dan Kimball, author of
They Like Jesus But Not The Church

Wesley Hill graciously offers himself in *Washed and Waiting.* He holds on to faith and hope while describing his own dark night of the soul as a gay man committed to the church's long-standing position of abstinence outside of heterosexual marriage. Straight people gain an empathetic understanding of homosexuality, and gay and lesbian Christians committed to celibacy will find a companion who identifies with their pain and loneliness. We are all reminded of the challenges associated with our striving for intimacy, sexual purity, and wholeness. A worthy read.

Lisa Graham McMinn, PhD, professor, George Fox

University, and author of Sexuality and Holy Longing

How do the gospel, holiness, and indwelling sin play out in the life of a Christian struggling with same-sex attraction? And how do brothers and sisters in Christ show love to them? Wesley Hill offers wise counsel that is biblically faithful, theologically serious, and oriented to the life and practice of the church. He accomplishes a number of things in this small book: a capable defense of the Christian tradition's prohibition of homosexual practice, an illuminating analysis of the isolating effects of struggle with this particular sin, a careful consideration of the present and future aspects of salvation, and a heartfelt call to fight for each other's faith and repentance as a church body. This is now *the* book regarding a crucial theological issue of our time.

Michael Allen, assistant professor of systematic theology,
Knox Theological Seminary

To my fellow Christians
who wrestle with their sexual identity
and hope for their promised redemption

AUTHOR'S NOTE

Although the stories I tell in this book are true, in most cases (except where permission was granted) I've changed the names and identifying details of the people mentioned. In at least one instance, I've created a composite character, based on several relationships and conversations I've had. All of this is in the interest of guarding the privacy of friends who do not wish to have their stories made public.

ACKNOWLEDGMENTS

Finishing this book would not have been possible without the encouragement of many friends. I am deeply grateful to those who read chapters and, in some cases, an entire draft of the manuscript, and gave me constructive feedback: Wayne Martindale, Alex Kirk, David Lincicum, Brian and Kristin Tabb, Todd Wilson, Luke Neff, Agnieszka Tennant, DeWayne Stallings, David Sims, Walter Moberly, Misty Irons, Noah Dennis, Roger and Haley Scharf, Jono Linebaugh, and Kathryn Greene-McCreight.

A few friends went above and beyond the call of duty. Charlie Shepherd and Tommy Grimm were there for me in a way no one else was during the writing process. Alan Jacobs not only read and commented insightfully but also put me in touch with others who helped move the project from rough manuscript to published book. Mardi Keyes believed in this book from the beginning; without her and the morning we spent together talking it over, I'm not sure I would have had the courage to move ahead toward publication. She went through the entire manuscript three times with a fine-toothed comb and made numerous helpful suggestions for improving it. Michael and Emily Allen were unfailing in their friendship, prayerfulness, and ability to give wise counsel. At later stages, Denis and Margie Haack, Abraham Piper, and Madison Trammel kept me convinced that this book deserved to see the light of day, and they helped make it happen, in concrete ways. Dan Treier, John Wilson, and Lil Copan gave generously of their time to help me understand and navigate the publishing process.

For spiritual direction, theological and pastoral oversight, and prayer, without which my life, and hence this book, would be immeasurably poorer, I am grateful to Scott Hafemann, Mark Talbot, Todd Augustine, Tom and Julie Steller, David Michael, Dan and Liz Holst, Chris Mitchell, and Ross and Barbie Anderson. Above all, I'm thankful for the constant, self-giving love of my family, my parents, sister and brother-in-law, and brother.

Any missteps—spiritual, theological, pastoral, or otherwise—are, of course, my own. Without the people mentioned here, there would be many more such missteps than there are already.

Lastly, I'm especially grateful to my editor, Ryan Pazdur, and Dirk Buursma, Chris Fann, and the rest of the team at Zondervan for believing in the message of this book and taking a risk on a first-time author.

INTRODUCTION

By the time I started high school, two things had become clear to me. One was that I was a Christian. My parents had raised me to be a believer in Jesus, and as I moved toward independence from my family, I knew that I wanted to remain one—that I wanted to trust, love, and obey Christ, who had been crucified and raised from the dead "for us and for our salvation," as the creed puts it. The second thing was that I was gay. For as long as I could remember, I had been drawn, even as a child, to other males in some vaguely confusing way, and after puberty, I had come to realize that I had a steady, strong, unremitting, exclusive sexual attraction to persons of the same sex.

Since that time of self-discovery, I have struggled week in and week out to know how to live faithfully as a Christian who experiences same-sex attraction. In the most difficult hours of that struggle, I have looked for articles or books to help me. I have searched for things written in the furnace, so to speak, by other gay Christians—books born out of intense personal wrestling with homosexuality, as well as with the demands of the gospel—that I could look to for guidance. I have found dozens, maybe hundreds, of scholarly articles and monographs debating the passages in the Bible that deal with homosexuality. Journals and encyclopedias gave me countless studies of the "psychosomatic," social, and possible genetic origins of homosexuality. Books of history and sociology detailed the ways various cultures and time periods have described and dealt with people who experience sexual desire for others of the same sex. But I have never found a book I could resonate with that tries to put into words some of the confusion and sorrow and triumph and grief and joy of the struggle to live faithfully before God, in Christ, with others, as a gay person. This is my attempt to write such a book.[1]

My story is very different from other stories told by people wearing the same designation—"homosexual Christian"—that I wear. Many in the church—more so in the mainline denominations than the evangelical ones, though that could soon change—tell stories of "homosexual holiness." The authors of these narratives profess a deep faith in Christ and claim a powerful experience of the Holy Spirit precisely *in* and *through*

---

[1]   As I was preparing this introduction, I came across the following comment by Philip Yancey: "Much of what I read on depression, on doubt, on suicide, on suffering, on homosexuality, seems written by people who begin with a Christian conclusion and who have never been through the anguished steps familiar to a person struggling with depression, doubt, suicide, suffering, or homosexuality. No resolution could be so matter-of-fact to a person who has actually survived such a journey." I hope in what follows to convey something of what it's like to have survived—or, rather, to be surviving—the anguished journey of struggling with homosexuality.

their homosexual practice. According to these Christians, their homosexuality is an expression of holiness, a symbol and conduit of God's grace in their lives.[2] My own story, by contrast, is a story of feeling spiritually hindered rather than helped by my homosexuality. Another way to say it would be to observe that my story testifies to the truth of the position the Christian church has held with almost total unanimity throughout the centuries—namely, that homosexuality was not God's original creative intention for humanity, that it is, on the contrary, a tragic sign of human nature and relationships being fractured by sin, and therefore that homosexual practice goes against God's express will for all human beings, especially those who trust in Christ.

But my story also differs from the one told by many others in the church, primarily evangelical believers. Unlike some, I have never experienced a dramatic, healing reversal of my homosexual desires. In other words, God's presence in my life has not meant that I have become heterosexual. Like Paul, I have prayed fervently, desperately, tearfully on multiple occasions for God to take away this "thorn in my flesh." I have listened to Christians who were formerly involved in gay and lesbian relationships testify to experiencing an extraordinary, decisive change in their sexual attractions and a newfound ability to live in normal marriages, free to a large extent from homoerotic inclinations. Chad Thompson, for example, in his book *Loving Homosexuals as Jesus*

Would, describes a road trip to Colorado with two male friends his own age who, by pouring out a steady stream of affirmation and nonerotic physical affection on Chad, became God's agents for healing the wounds that were at the root of Chad's homoerotic desires.[3] Although I don't want to dispute that this is evidence of the love, grace, and power of God, and without wanting to diminish anyone's hope in God's ability to change homosexual desires in this way (for some), I do want to say that this has not been my experience. Nor has it been the experience of many gay and lesbian Christians who are silently struggling to remain faithful as they worship and serve with us, day after day, in the fellowship of the church.

So this book is neither about how to live faithfully as a practicing homosexual person nor about how to live faithfully as a fully healed or former homosexual man or woman. J.I. Packer, commenting on Paul's hopeful word for sexual sinners in 1 Corinthians 6:9–11, writes, "With some of the Corinthian Christians, Paul was celebrating the moral empowering of the Holy Spirit in heterosexual terms; with others of the Corinthians, today's homosexuals are called to prove, live out, and celebrate the moral empowering of the Holy Spirit in homosexual terms."[4] This book is about what it means to do that—how, practically, a nonpracticing but still-desiring homosexual Christian can "prove, live out, and celebrate" the grace of Christ and the power of the Holy Spirit *in homosexual terms.*

This book is written mainly for those gay Christians who are already convinced that their discipleship to Jesus necessarily commits them to the demanding, costly obedience of choosing not to nurture their homosexual desires, whether through private fantasies or physical relationships with other gay or lesbian people. According to Martin Hallett, himself a homosexual Christian who leads a ministry to gay and lesbian persons in the United Kingdom called True Freedom Trust, "There are probably nearly as many Christians with homosexual feelings who do not believe that homosexual sex is right for Christians as there are those who are advocating its acceptance."[5] He goes on to write:

A friend of mine in Sweden (Erik) is a Lutheran priest who believes in the traditional biblical teaching on sexuality and has homosexual feelings himself. He determined, from the beginning of his call to the ordained ministry, that he would be open about his sexuality at every stage.... Ultimately, as more evangelicals make such a public stand, it will seem less costly and will, I believe, have a tremendous impact for the kingdom of God....

[I want to] encourage those leaders in the church who have homosexual feelings but who believe homosexual sex is wrong to be more open. People like Erik ... are not a tiny minority in terms of all homosexuals in the church.... I wish their voice could be heard, saying that "we believe our homosexuality is part of our value and giftedness to the church, but homosexual sex is a sin." What a difference this would make to the life, witness, and future of the body of Christ.[6]

With Hallett and his friend Erik, I want to contribute in some small way to breaking the silence that persists in many churches. It is no secret that a large number of gay Christians feel frightened at the thought of sharing the story of their sexuality with their fellow believers. Those who do bring their struggle to the light often confess that for years they kept it under wraps out of fear and shame. Far from wanting to contribute in any way to this widespread sense of shame, I hope this book may encourage other homosexual Christians to take the risky step of opening up their lives to others in the body of Christ. In so doing, they may find, as I have, by grace, that being known is spiritually healthier than remaining behind closed doors, that the light is better than the darkness.

While writing these reflections, I have often thought of a scene from Richard Attenborough's *Shadowlands,* a powerful film about the love affair between C.S. Lewis and Joy Davidman. At the very end of the film, Lewis has passed through the worst throes of his grief over Joy's recent death from cancer. He has held on to his faith in God, but he seems older, more world-weary, and more jaded by easy solutions to what he had earlier termed the "problem of pain." "I have no answers anymore," he says, "only the life I have lived." In many ways, I feel similarly about what I have written in the pages that follow. At the end of the day, the only "answer" I have to offer to the question of how to live well before God and with others as a homosexual Christian is the life I am trying to live by the power of the gospel.

In my late twenties, I still feel very young and in need of growth, both in my understanding of Christian discipleship and of human sexuality. There are still avenues of possible healing that I want to explore, and I hope to receive more counseling and spiritual direction in the future. But for that reason, because I am still in the midst of an agonizing and confusing period of trying to forge an identity for myself as a Christian who wrestles with homosexuality, I may be able to offer a helpful perspective for others like me who know without a doubt that they want to follow Jesus and who at the same time struggle day in and day out with homosexual desires.

Mainly, then, I am writing as one homosexual Christian for other homosexual Christians. I am writing for those who have grown up feeling like resident aliens and have struggled to know why. I am writing for gay and lesbian Christians who fear what their parents might think when they discover the attractions their sons or daughters have wrestled with for years. I'm writing for those gay and lesbian Christians who married heterosexuals in a lastditch effort to change their sexual orientation but who find their homosexual desires just as strong today as they ever were before.

I have in mind all the gay and lesbian Christians living behind closed doors, desperately wanting to share their deepest secret with the churches they attend but feeling unable to. I am writing for people in their late twenties or even thirties or forties and beyond who, for the first time in their lives, are experiencing the awakening of homosexual impulses and desires and are scared to death as to what they might mean and how to deal with them. I am writing for gay and lesbian persons who have experienced stinging rejections from Christians but who nevertheless are convinced that God wants them to try to live pure and faithful lives within the flawed and often hurtful community of the church. I am writing for homosexual persons who have tried—and are trying—to "become heterosexual" and are not succeeding and wonder, for the umpteenth time, what exactly it is that God wants them to do.

But I also have in mind others—parents, brothers and sisters, close relatives not in the immediate family, good friends, pastors, youth leaders, counselors—who are close to homosexual Christians and want to help guide them toward healing, wholeness, and Christian maturity. I hope that they, too, will read this book and benefit from reflecting on the experiences I describe.

And I hope there are others who will "overhear" what I write who struggle long and hard with persistent, unwanted desires or other afflictions that are similar in some ways to those of gay and lesbian

Christians—chemical dependencies, eating disorders, mental and emotional disturbances of various kinds. If Christians in these and other related positions are able to adapt and appropriate some of what I say to fit their own situations, I will be happy. The Christian's struggle with homosexuality is unique in many ways but not completely so. The dynamics of human sinfulness and divine mercy and grace are the same for all of us, regardless of the particular temptations or weaknesses we face.

***

In my experience, the effort to live faithfully as a gay Christian has involved me in three main battles. First has been the struggle to understand what exactly the gospel demands of homosexual Christians; why it seems to require that I not act on my homosexual desires—and how the gospel enables me to actually fulfill this demand. Chapter 1 of this book, "A Story-Shaped Life," is devoted to these questions.

Second, for me, being a Christian who experiences intense homoerotic desires has meant loneliness—feelings of isolation, fears that I will be alone all my life with my brokenness, that no one will be there for the long haul to walk this road with me. Most gay Christians who are convinced that gay sex isn't an option will, I suspect, probably find celibacy to be the best or only alternative for living in a way that is faithful to the gospel's call for purity. And because of that, most gay Christians will experience loneliness. So the question becomes: How do we live with this loneliness? Is there any relief for it? What comforts does the gospel offer? This is the focus of chapter 2, "The End of Loneliness."

Finally, in my life and in the lives of many others, shame has been a constant struggle in the effort to live out the life of Christ and his Spirit in homosexual terms. Guilt over homosexual sin, a nagging, unshakable feeling of being "damaged goods," a sense of being broken beyond repair—and therefore of being regularly, unavoidably displeasing to God—these all seem endemic to much homosexual Christian experience. In chapter 3, "The Divine Accolade," I address this struggle and try to express the conviction that has become the heartbeat of my life—that we homosexual Christians, in the words of C.S. Lewis, can actually be "a real ingredient in the divine happiness."[7] We can please God, can truly experience his pleasure in the midst of sexual brokenness, and in the end share in his glory.

Interspersed throughout these chapters are three mini-biographies or character sketches of homosexual Christians. The first is my own life story, and I have also included the stories of Henri Nouwen, the now-deceased gay Catholic writer on spirituality, and the nineteenth-century homoerotically inclined Jesuit poet Gerard Manley Hopkins, in the hope that hearing about the travails and triumphs of three real-life homosexual Christians may help readers put hands and feet on the more theoretical material in the main chapters of the book.

It is my prayer that God may use the reflections in this book to help others live faithfully before him until the time when he makes all things new. Until then, we *wait* in hope (Romans 8:25), *washed* clean by his Son and Spirit (1 Corinthians 6:11).

***

Before moving on, I want to briefly describe the terminology used in the following pages. In this book I have chosen not to discriminate between various terms for homosexuality. So, for instance, I use "same-sex attraction," "homosexual desires," "homosexuality," and related terms interchangeably. Likewise, I've used a variety of designations for gay and lesbian people. Instead of sticking to one term, such as "homosexual Christian," I also refer to myself as a "gay Christian" or "a Christian who experiences homosexual desires." These phrases are all synonymous for me, and though they are open to misunderstanding, in my judgment the gains in using them outweigh the potential hazards. None of them should be taken necessarily to imply homosexual practice; in each case I am most often placing the emphasis on the subject's sexual orientation and not the corresponding behavior.

There is, however, one way of speaking that I've tried to avoid. Rather than refer to someone as "a homosexual," I've taken care always to make "gay" homosexual" the adjective, and never the noun, in a longer phrase, such as "gay Christian" or "homosexual person." In this way, I hope to send a subtle linguistic signal that being gay isn't the most important thing about my or any other gay person's identity. I am a *Christian* before I am anything else. My homosexuality is a part of my makeup, a facet of my personality. One day, I believe, whether in this life or in the resurrection, it will fade away. But my identity as a Christian—someone incorporated into Christ's body by his Spirit—will remain.

PART ONE PRELUDE

WASHED AND WAITING

WASHED AND WAITING

You were washed, you were sanctified, you were justified in the name of the Lord Jesus Christ and by the Spirit of our God.

1 Corinthians 6:11

We ourselves, who have the firstfruits of the Spirit, groan inwardly as we wait eagerly for adoption as sons, the redemption of our bodies.... If we hope for what we do not see, we wait for it with patience.

Romans 8:23, 25

Puberty came late for me, or so it felt at the time. I was almost thirteen years old, but far from being the exciting whirlwind of change that it was for my friends, the experience terrified me. From the very beginning of those unsettling months, I found strange new desires—it wasn't clear to me then that they were sexual—for the other guys my age who were going through the same turbulent transformation. I started noticing and being fascinated by the firming muscles and the growing hair of my male friends. I would steal glances at them whenever I could, trying not to be caught but unsure why I felt it necessary to be so secretive.

I remember being at an airport once for a field trip my church group took to the air traffic control tower. At some point, several friends of mine slipped away from the hawkish gaze of our teachers and started exploring the airport's souvenir shops and magazine racks. I jogged with them along one of the terminals, feeling rebellious and carefree, laughing. In one of the shops, they found *Playboy* magazines. They were in plain view on a shelf along the back wall, and one of my friends quickly opened one as the rest of us huddled around, ducking out of the salesclerk's line of sight. In an instant I felt like an outsider. I wouldn't have been able to express it at the time, but I realized something was different. I felt no rush, no thrill, no curiosity, no sense of the mysterious attraction that my friends all seemed to be relishing as they glanced nervously over their shoulders until the clerk saw us and angrily ordered us out of the shop.

In those tingly days of growing into a new kind of body, I wasn't sure why I had images of other *guys,* other males, parading through my excited yet faintly discomfited mind. Maybe all this was part of the process of growing up and would go away eventually? I didn't speculate too much about it all—I didn't know enough to ask good questions. Mostly I tried to weather what felt like a strange but soon-to-pass storm that was part guilty plea-sure, part confusing agony.

Around this time, my parents made the decision that we should stop attending the large Southern Baptist church where we were members. I had not yet entered the youth group at that church and really had no desire to. I felt mortified by the pimples covering my temples, nose, and chin, and whenever I tried to talk to someone else my own age, I could feel my face turning a hot shade of red and my armpits sweating. I had spent my entire life up to that point in a sheltered Southern fundamentalism and would have preferred never to have a conversation with any peer if I could help it. My parents found a smaller, nondenominational church with a dozen kids in the youth group, most of whom I knew already and felt more at ease around, and we made the switch.

During the next three years, I grew out of much of the scared awkwardness of those first months of puberty. But changing churches and becoming less socially inept didn't make one iota's difference when it came to my sexuality. I still felt in my gut that something had gone wrong. Somehow genetic wires must have been crossed, and as a result there had been a glitch in my otherwise normal development.

As I left childhood behind and began to learn more about myself and the world I lived in, I came to realize that what had happened to my mind and body was drastically different from what had happened to my friends'. When I started meeting with a small group of guys at my church for prayer and accountability, lust was, predictably, one of the main topics of discussion. "We like to mentally undress girls we see—what should we do about that?" one of us maturely asked our twentysomething leader. "Come on, we're all red-blooded American males here," another one of the guys chimed in. "We can talk about our struggles openly." I came to realize, with a mild sense of panic, that I *couldn't* talk about *my* struggle openly—couldn't identify with my friends as they discussed their frustrations with knowing how to handle their hormones. My problem was never mentally undressing *girls.* As they talked, I planned how to keep my answers vague so that my difference would remain a secret.

***

My earliest childhood memories are of my mother reading colorful, rhyming Bible storybooks to me and helping me draw pictures with crayons of my favorite Bible characters. I understood at a very young age that Jesus had died on a cross, condemned by the Jewish high priests and the Roman government in Jerusalem, and that after lying three days in a tomb, he had risen from the dead. Growing up, I never doubted that this was, somehow, the most important news in the world and that it could be the center of people's lives because I saw that it was the center of my parents' lives. I prayed at a young age, in good evangelical fashion, to "ask Jesus into my heart." I was baptized at age eleven.

By the time I reached the ninth grade or so, I had been fully persuaded that Jesus was and is God come in the flesh for me and for my salvation, and I knew I wanted to spend the rest of my life loving and obeying him. Over time, my parents' nurturing role was replaced by my own reading of the Bible. In a process filled with starts and stops, I learned to pray, to dialogue with God on my own, as I drove my car or lay in my bed at night. I read books on spirituality and doctrine by C.S. Lewis, Frederick Buechner, J.I. Packer, Henri Nouwen, and John Piper. Self-motivated now, I started wrestling with the perennial problems of Christian discipleship. I looked for answers in the Bible and asked my youth pastor lots of questions over barbecue sandwiches and Cokes at a local greasy spoon.

Birdlike, I was testing my wings, coming of age. But at the same time that I was learning to engage with God as a hungry, growing young Christian, the realization dawned on me like a dead weight sinking in my stomach that no amount of spiritual growth seemed to have any effect on my sexual preference. The homoerotic attractions I had been conscious of since waking up to the strange new universe of sexuality remained so constant and unbroken that I came to realize I was experiencing what was usually called "homosexuality." I had a homosexual orientation. I was gay.

For me, admitting this to myself—I have memories of lying in bed, staring at the ceiling in the dark, mulling it over, forming the word *homosexual* silently on my lips—was like an awareness that steals up on you one day out of the blue. It was there all along, but you saw it just then. There was nothing, it felt, *chosen* or *intentional* about my being gay. It seemed more like noticing the blueness of my eyes than deciding I would take up skiing. There was never an option—"Do you want to be gay?" "Yes, I do, please." It was a gradual coming to terms, not a conscious resolution.

I remember listening to James Dobson's *Focus on the Family* radio broadcast occasionally with my mother as we rode somewhere in the car together. My ears would perk up when the subject of homosexuality came up, which it did often, since this was the mid-1990s, and the "gay rights" movement was gaining steam. Dobson talked a lot about the "causes" of homosexuality—childhood sexual abuse, an emotionally distant father, the absence of affectionate male role models. I remember scrutinizing my past and present experiences. Did I fit these categories? I had never been sexually abused by anyone, let alone my parents. Was I close enough to my dad? I *could* think of one time I tried to initiate a weekly time for just the two of us to be together, but it flopped. Plus, I never learned to play golf with him, nor did I want to take up deer hunting, as he seemed to hope I would. Did that mean I was suffering from a lack of paternal intimacy? I wracked my brain for answers, testing every possible explanatory avenue to understand how I came to have the homoerotic feelings that blazed like a fire in my head every day.

From time to time, not often, I would experiment with different strategies for awakening heterosexual desire. The lingerie section of the catalogs my mom received in the mail never did anything for me. The curves of women's bodies on TV or movie screens flickered past my gaze with so little attraction that most of the time I didn't give them a second thought.

One afternoon during my high school years, sitting on my bed in my room with the door closed, I was reading Elie Wiesel's novel *Dawn* and came to a passage where Wiesel described two characters about to have sex. The girl was dressed in a blouse with no bra, and the man kissing her could see her breasts. I reread the passage several times, my face flushed with shame, trying to force some awakening of desire. I felt a faint stirring of excitement that, at the time, seemed unprecedented and earth-shattering. I stumbled off my bed, trembling slightly. I think that was the only time I have ever experienced sexual desire for a woman's body, and it was so slight that, looking back, I sometimes wonder if maybe it was only a dream.

All through high school I never once even considered the possibility of pursuing a full-fledged homosexual relationship. I didn't know any other gay people, and besides that, I was too steeped in the conservative, fundamentalist Christian world of the Bible Belt to consider a gay partnership to be a live option. All I had heard about homosexuality up to that point was that it was a sin, that God never made anyone homosexual, and that he wanted those who were homosexual to follow some regimen of "reparative therapy" so that they could become decisively heterosexual.

I told no one about my homosexual feelings, not even my family, whom I was unusually close to in many ways. My strategy for coping with my condition was ignoring it, turning a blind eye to it, stuffing it deep into dark recesses of my consciousness and hoping that eventually it would be so deeply buried it would die for lack of exposure.

***

The fall of my senior year of high school, I began the process of applying to colleges. I got accepted to Wheaton College, a Christian liberal arts school near Chicago, and decided to go. As the time drew near to start college, I wondered what role my homosexuality would play in the experience. Would I meet a girl, as many people did at college, and would this miraculously alter my orientation? Mostly I strategized about how to keep my homosexuality under wraps. Imaginatively playing out different scenarios that could happen in the dorm, with roommates, in the community showers, and on the sports fields, I felt reasonably sure I could avoid being found out if I were careful.

My time at Wheaton turned out to be more fun and fruitful and stretching and horizon expanding than I could have guessed. I grew personally, spiritually, and academically by leaps and bounds. I was happily stunned by the feeling of being a fish that has finally plopped into its home pool after flapping in the air, gills gulping for it doesn't know what.

One of the first classes I took my freshman year was on Christianity and culture, and for the final assignment, I chose to write a paper on a Christian view of homosexuality. I felt vaguely nervous doing so. Would people guess at my reason for choosing this topic and grow suspicious?

Writing this paper gave me the excuse I had been looking for to read a little of what theologians, philosophers, sociologists, psychologists, and psychiatrists were saying about homosexuality. For the first time, I read about the possible genetic origins of homosexuality. The dialectic of "nature and nurture," the debate over "essentialism" versus "constructivism," and the figures of the Kinsey report opened up new vistas of unexplored questions about my own experiences with homoerotic attraction. I discovered that there were serious, thoughtful, godly, and grace-filled Christians who thought, in many cases, that whatever degree of "construction" and "nurture" had conspired with genetic or chemical or hormonal hardwiring to produce a homosexual orientation, such an orientation was almost impossible to change.

But in my reading I also discovered that by far the majority of Christians—on the basis of their reading of several key passages from the Bible, together with the weight of Christian tradition, Catholic, Orthodox, and Protestant—agreed that homosexual *practice* was sinful. Having gay sex was off-limits. Christians talked regularly, I found, of God's original intention for creation and that, indeed, God, strictly speaking, didn't *make* anyone homosexual. Rather, homosexuality was one of myriad tragic consequences of living in a fallen world stalked by the specters of sin and death.

As I read and thought about homosexuality throughout my four years of college, I felt that the things I had learned in writing my initial paper—as amateur as it was—were confirmed. Somehow, in some way, I would have to be faithful to this Christian conviction—that homosexual lust, fantasies, and practice, whether self-stimulated or in partnership with another person, gay or straight, were not God's will for my life. The question for me became, then: Could I change and become heterosexual? I had, of course, wondered this before. But instead of trying to keep my homosexual feelings under wraps, maybe now was the time to try in earnest, with concerted effort, to invert them.

***

> In remembrance resides the secret of redemption.
>
> *Baal Shem Tov, founder of Hasidism*

Slowly, almost imperceptibly, during college my homosexual orientation started to become more central to my self-understanding. I remember once being in the basement bathroom of my sophomore dorm and seeing scrawled in tiny script on the inside of one of the toilet stalls: "Gay at Wheaton—you are not alone" with an email address underneath it. I felt my throat tighten and sensed simultaneously an affinity with and aversion to the nameless writer. I wasn't like him, I told myself, and yet I *was* like him. We were somehow related, companions on the same path.

In conversations with roommates, whenever the topic of dating came up (as it did with unsurprising regularity), I would chime in with names of girls I pretended to find myself romantically attracted to. My sophomore year, I took a girl out to a concert—my first date ever—and it felt awkward and strained. I was relieved when I dropped her off at her dorm.

But the following year, I met a girl whom I was shocked to find myself genuinely interested in. I quickly got past a false first impression that she was distant and aloof, and I started looking for natural, unforced ways to hang out with her—casual phone chats, long lunches together in our college dining commons, late-night talks after meetings with the

14

discipleship team we were both members of. After each conversation, I found myself wondering if maybe this would be the remedy I had been looking for, the solution to the problem of my homosexuality. I started praying earnestly and frequently that God would bring us together, that something beautiful and lasting would work out between us. When she finally told me she was interested in another guy, I went back to my apartment and cried harder than I had in years.

During the same year, my friend Jenna, one of the most free-spirited and life-giving people I knew at the time, started battling depression. I didn't find out about her struggle until months after she had found help and was recovering well. Over lunch one day, Jenna described that dark time and told me something that has remained with me ever since: "I just wanted to be whole again, Wes, and I thought that by pretending it wasn't there, the depression would just go away. But ignoring is not the path to redeeming. If I wanted this depression to be redeemed, I had to face it head-on." I tried to swallow the lump in my throat, realizing those words were for me. *Ignoring is not the path to redeeming.*

I knew that the time had come to seek help. My attempts to stuff my sexuality away somewhere, while at the same time paradoxically trying to "fix" it through some spark-filled, magical romance with a girl, were not working. But who should I talk to? I quickly ruled out my family. Though loving and sensitive, they were still very conservative. What would they think if their near-perfect firstborn admitted to being gay, even if he did make it clear he was abstinent? I also ruled out my roommates; it would be too confusing and difficult to try to explain away all the masks I had worn and tell them that, no, I really wasn't quite attracted to all those girls I talked about in the way that they thought I was.

I finally decided to talk to my philosophy professor, who seemed to be the wisest person I knew at the time. He not only could talk intelligently about the Enlightenment and postmodernism, but he knew about *life,* about the angst and existential struggles of college students like me, "about what it is to be human and hungry in a fallen world full of wonders," to use Barbara Brown Taylor's haunting phrase.[1] He seemed to have a genuine, growing trust in God, moving naturally and effortlessly in class from discussing Locke and Hume to talking about his love for Scripture and his struggles to believe in God's sovereignty and goodness in the midst of his own partial paralysis. He was constantly giving us interesting advice that made us roll our eyes in the moment and turn it over and over in our minds long afterward as we lay in our dorm rooms in the dark.

I remember one class discussion in particular when he told us with disarming openness about an experience he had had years earlier. "I once faced a temptation that was so persistent and so overwhelming that I literally believed my whole world would go dark if I refused to give in to it," he said. "All I could do was scream to the Holy Spirit to keep me from it." I knew at that point that, at the very least, this professor would understand my struggle better than anyone else I could think of, and with a nervously beating heart, I pounded out a vague email asking if maybe, at some point, possibly—that is, only if he had the time, of course—could he and I meet to talk about something really important to me? After several failed attempts at getting together, we finally settled on a time to meet in his office.

When the afternoon arrived, my heart was beating so hard it felt like it might explode out of my chest. More than once, I considered bringing up some other topic for discussion once I got there and pretending that it had been the reason for my visit all along. The walk from my apartment to main campus west along College Avenue took about ten minutes, and I remember a strange feeling of inevitability, as if there was no turning back, as I squinted against the bitter Chicago wind. Someone—the first person in the world—was finally going to know my biggest secret. I *wanted* to do this, and yet I wasn't ready. Maybe I could hold off a year or two more and my homosexuality would mysteriously disappear and no one would ever have to know?

I got to the professor's office on the fourth floor of Blanchard Hall, and as we made small talk, my words started to slur, as if I had had a piece of ice in my mouth for too long that had numbed my tongue. "Well," I eventually began, swallowing and choking, "there's something I want to tell you. I think I've been *needing* to tell someone about this, and I don't know who else to talk to—"

There were no fireworks, no prophetic, life-altering message, no tears on my part, no liberating sense of floating on air for having bared my soul. After I finished, the professor thanked me for telling him. "I want you to know that I will begin praying for you regularly, Wes," he said. We went on to talk about the possible causes of my homosexuality (he wondered if genes played some role), and whether—and in what form—I should expect "healing." I'm not sure what exactly I was hoping the outcome of our talk would be, but when I left the meeting, I felt a mingled sense of relief— *I'm not alone in knowing this about myself anymore!* —and dread— *The road ahead is too long and hard!* There were no easy solutions, no quick fixes, and oceans of confusion and struggle I would have to navigate.

***

A few weeks later, the professor wrote to tell me about a psychologist friend of his who had counseled many homosexual persons and researched and written extensively on homosexuality from an explicitly Christian point of view. Would I be interested in meeting with him? Yes, I said, I would like to do that. The professor called and set up the appointment for me. When I got to the psychologist's office on

Wheaton's campus, his secretary welcomed me warmly. Slightly paranoid, I wondered if she knew why I had come. Did her eyes betray any awareness of my "situation"? Sitting down opposite her desk while I waited for him to finish a phone conversation, I looked through the narrow window in the door and watched students wearing backpacks jostle past, laughing and talking in between classes. I thought, *I sure hope no one who knows me looks in and sees me here. What excuse will I give for why I'm in* this *office?*

In our meeting, my professor's friend instantly put me at ease. His whole demeanor exuded kindness, grace, and dignity. I realized quickly that the professor had not told him why I wanted to meet with him; he had said only that I was asking some earnest, heart-searching questions about my life and that he thought the psychologist could help. As I began to tell some of my story, the psychologist's brow creased in concern; I felt listened to and cared for. "Having heard all this," I concluded, "do you think there's any possibility for change? What should my next step in this journey be?"

We talked about many things that afternoon. It wasn't exactly a counseling session—"If that were the case, I would be listening more and speaking a lot less," he said with a warm smile. But I came away with fresh perspectives and new insights. "If I could leave you with an encouragement, it would be this," he said toward the end of our time together: "*Be spiritually adventuresome."* I have thought about this on many occasions since that meeting—thought about it more often than acted on it probably, but it has remained with me as a ringing challenge. "Don't be afraid to pursue multiple avenues for healing," he said. "God has used everything from charismatic deliverance ministries to support groups to professional therapists to contemplative spiritual directors to guide homosexual Christians toward wholeness. Maybe one or more of these avenues is for you. If God directs you to one, step out in faith. Don't let your background or commitment to your own tradition"—I thought of my fundamentalist upbringing and wondered if his words were more relevant than he guessed—"make you fearful of joining in the adventure the Holy Spirit prepares for you."

After that meeting, my eyes were peeled. What avenues of healing did God want to take me down?

***

This is perhaps the hardest truth of any to grasp. Do we wake up every morning amazed that we are loved by God?

David Ford, The Shape of Living

Near the start of my senior year, in August, I became friends with a girl named Tara. She had already graduated from Wheaton and moved across the country, so most of our interaction was via email. By October, we were writing long letters to each other, exploring random, rambling trails of thought, swapping stories from childhood and adolescence, and commiserating on the same existential quandaries. Looking back, it was pretty heady stuff for a college senior.

Early on in our correspondence, I wondered what was happening. I didn't *like* Tara—in *that* sense that I had faked before with other girls. I wasn't romantically attracted to her, or at least I didn't think so. Could I be? Is there such a thing for a gay man as romantic attraction to a woman? I didn't know. As I sat in my tiny, second-story bedroom, I clicked the Send button in Microsoft Outlook every night and wondered.

Tara and I tried to share with each other who we were. We talked about our families, our upbringings; we talked about our hopes for the next few years of our lives, our desires for what we wanted to be and to do. In one of her very first letters, Tara told me about her work one summer in San Francisco for a street ministry to male prostitutes. The ministry owned a couple of buildings on a block in the heart of the city, and she worked in the one that served as a kind of shelter for guys coming in off the street who needed a hot meal and people to talk to. "I'm not sure why," Tara said in reflecting on her time at the street ministry, "but God has given me a concern for gay people. Homosexuality is not something I or anyone in my family has struggled with, but God has just put on my heart the people who do struggle with it." When I initially read those words, I was confused. Was God doing something here in my friendship with Tara that was bigger than I had anticipated? Could this be some sort of "sign"?

I decided, perhaps wrongly, not to talk to Tara about my homosexuality. And unsurprisingly, the romance I'd hoped for didn't spring up between us. But I think of my friendship with Tara as a milestone on my journey. Painfully, threateningly (or so it felt at the time), Tara put her finger on a resistance to God's love I didn't know I was harboring. (I have since learned that many gay Christians wrestle with feelings of isolation, shame, and guilt that lead them to question God's love for them or simply feel cold and calloused to it.) Through Tara's emails, I came to see that my identity was rooted more in "having all my ducks in a row" and less in a personal sense of *belonging,* of being included in "the Beloved," as Paul puts it in Ephesians 1:6, of being healed and made whole through God's cherishing care.

Once Tara described an experience she had had while studying in England for a semester. She had been striving to understand and be what she thought she *should* understand and be. Finally one night, in a ser-vice at Coventry Cathedral, she relaxed and submitted to God's wound-mending embrace. She felt that God loved her just as she was. I read Tara's description of that night at Coventry several times, and I realized, with a cold, smarting sense of mingled sadness and helplessness, that I knew very little, firsthand, of what she was describing. My first thought as I got out of bed every morning was not, *I am the beloved of God.* I had not mastered the discipline, as N.T. Wright calls it, of looking to the cross of Christ and seeing evidence there that I am loved extravagantly and inexorably by the self-giving triune God.

Tara's emails proved to be crucial for me. It has taken years for me to learn, bit by bit, this spiritual practice of meditating on the love of God and to understand that it is central to my struggle with homosexuality. I mark my correspondence with Tara as the time when I consciously began the daily effort to view myself as God's beloved, redeemed by the self-gift of Christ.

But I also look back on my short-lived attraction to Tara (I had never been sexually aroused by her) as the time that showed me, once and for all, I could not count on a relationship with a woman to magically reverse my sexual orientation. Healing, if it ever came on this side of God's future, would have to take a different form.

✳✳✳

By then it was clear to me that I needed something more in this struggle to know how to live well as a Christian with homosexual desires. No one I lived with or talked to on a daily basis knew about my struggle, and it was no secret to me that this wasn't ideal. So I decided to approach one of my pastors and ask him if he would be willing to meet with me on a weekly basis, "for prayer and accountability," even though I still wasn't sure what it would be realistic to hope for.

Denny was already an acquaintance when, one Sunday before the worship ser-vice started, he spotted me sliding into a pew near the front of the sanctuary, caught my eye, and, smiling, wandered over to give me a firm handshake and see how I had been doing. We chatted for a bit as the organist started pumping out the prelude, and then, screwing up my courage, I asked Denny if he and I could talk one-on-one sometime soon, maybe over lunch or a cup of coffee.

When the time arrived, I showed up at his office at the church and repeated what was starting to feel like a familiar routine. I told him a lot of what I had said to my philosophy professor and the Wheaton psychologist and then said, "Even though I'm not alone in this anymore, even though I finally told someone about this, I feel like I need someone to talk to on a regular basis, someone who can help me sort things out, someone I can pray with."

Denny's eye contact was intense as I talked. His look was a mix of compassion and concern—and bewilderment. "So, Wes, can you help me understand this better?" he asked gently when I had finished. "What do you mean when you talk about homosexual desires?" I fumbled for an answer, and he tried to help with a concrete scenario: "For example, are you turned on when you watch a men's underwear commercial on TV?" I couldn't help but laugh inside. Denny was clearly unacquainted with what it would mean for someone to struggle with homosexuality. I answered that that could be part of it, yes, but it was so much bigger. Somehow every part of my relational makeup was affected by this. As I would later write in a letter to a friend, "A sexual orientation is such a complex and, in most cases, it seems, intractable thing; I for one cannot imagine what 'healing' from my orientation would look like, given that it seems to manifest itself not only in physical attraction to male bodies but also in a preference for male company, with all that it entails," such as conversation and emotional intimacy and quality time spent together.

"What I wish," I finally said to Denny, "is that I could feel the church to be a safe place. I've come to you because I know you and I trust you," I went on, "but even more than that, I've come to you because you're my pastor, and I want to see this whole church thing be what it's supposed to be. If you're willing and if you have the time, I'd love for you to *pastor* me."

After that, for most of the second semester of my senior year of college, Denny and I met once a week. We had a standing appointment: I would wander across the street from my house on campus to the church building, and we would make small talk for a few minutes, and then our conversations would turn serious. I confessed sin at those meetings. We talked about what it would mean for the church to truly support its homosexual Christian members.

At several of our meetings, Denny and I discussed recent statements by evangelical Christian leaders that I had found helpful. Gordon Hugenberger, the pastor of Park Street Church in Boston, for example, had recently written to his parishioners:

I do want to emphasize that I do *not* consider homosexuality to be worse than any of the zillion sins I commit every day. In fact, it is a tribute to the infinite grace and mercy of God that the sanctuary roof stays up each day that I walk into the room. In any case, we are not on some kind of crusade to single out those who may be dealing with this issue. Although I want the liberty to be honest with the Bible and to address this topic from time to time, I have no intention of so stressing it that the many homosexual guests and visitors who are not interested in changing will feel put off or unwelcome (or at least no more put off or unwelcome than the many materialists who are not yet interested in changing). On the other hand, I want to say enough so that those who are trying to surrender this part of their lives to Christ will be encouraged, and also so that the rest will not be misled by a culture that increasingly is allowing only one side of the discussion to be heard.[2]

Denny spent many hours trying to convince me that Hugenberger was right: my homosexual temptations weren't any more (or less) tragic than temptations to greed, pride, or anger that Christians face on a daily basis.

Denny and I also talked about a statement that Richard Bewes, rector of All Souls Church, London, a sister church to mine and Denny's, had made. The statement and what Denny said to me afterward sum up the spirit of our weekly times together.

We also wish warmly to affirm those sisters and brothers, already in membership with orthodox churches, who—while experiencing same-sex desires and feelings—nevertheless battle with the rest of us, in repentance and faith, for a lifestyle that affirms marriage [between a man and woman] and celibacy as the two given norms for sexual expression. There is room for every kind of background and past sinful experience among members of Christ's flock as we learn the way of repentance and renewed lives, for *Such were some of you. But you were washed, you were sanctified, you were justified in the name of the Lord Jesus Christ and by the Spirit of our God* (1 Corinthians 6:11).

This is true inclusivity.[3]

"They *get* it, don't they, Wes?" Denny said simply, smiling, when I had stopped reading and folded the piece of paper. "It's about warm affirmation. It's about battling together for holiness, in repentance and faith, on a daily basis. It's about the church being the church, as we *all* struggle toward wholeness."

***

"I don't know if you've shared your struggle with anyone else, but *if you haven't, you need to,*" I wrote recently to a fellow homosexual Christian. "Speaking from personal experience," I told him:

> I would encourage you to share it both with wise, older Christians who can speak from their maturity into your life but also with younger Christians who are your peers. I don't think I would have made it this far in my struggle with homosexuality had I not had the several close friends to whom I turn often for support, perspective, laughter (yes, it's *really* important in this battle, I think, to not get too heavy-hearted), encouragement, counsel, rebuke, warning, and—most of all—prayer. When I cannot feel God's love for me in my struggle, to have a friend grab my shoulder and say, "I love you, and I'm in this with you for the long haul" is, in some ways, an incarnation of God's love that I would otherwise have trouble resting in.

I could not have written those words in college because I hadn't told any peers about my struggle or experienced the kind of rich comfort and support I have since enjoyed. It was only after graduating and moving to Minneapolis to be involved in ministry at a large urban church that I would discover how crucial nonerotic friendships with peers of the same sex are in my pilgrimage toward wholeness.

At Denny's advice, soon after moving, I made an appointment to meet with one of the pastors of my new church (already a friend of mine of several years) to tell him about my sexual struggles. No more secrets. I had tasted something of what it meant to walk in the light, and I wanted more. I wanted more than anything to see the church be the church and to know what it can mean to feel the freedom of openness and the consolations of community.

In the following weeks, I also met with a counselor, which proved to be a turning point. He told me pointedly, "I would hate for you to come to a point, say, two years from now and look around at the friends you've made here and have to say, 'I never became close friends with any of them.'" Then, in a question that has haunted me ever since, he asked, "Do you find yourself holding other males at arm's length for fear that if you come to know them deeply and intimately, it will somehow be inappropriate or dangerous or uncomfortable?" I had never thought about this before, but as soon as he asked it, that question felt like a stab of hot, white light piercing some corner of my heart I hadn't known existed. I left that meeting feeling that I needed to find a guy friend—or two or three—my own age with whom I could share my secrets, who could walk this road with me.

One night, sitting on the dirty carpeted floor of the bedroom of a downtown bachelor pad in a circle of guys my age, I came very close to breaking down and asking them for help and for prayer. A black light was glowing from where it was attached to a corner of the bunk beds, incense was burning on a shelf, one of the guys was strumming a guitar, and we were all shooting the breeze after a spaghetti dinner. Knees tucked under my chin, I felt my heart start to pound and my palms grow sweaty when one of the guys brought up the topic of homosexuality: "Have any of you ever had a gay or lesbian friend?" Another one of the guys, Charlie, said yes, he had had a close friend in college who had wrestled with homosexual inclinations. "He and I would go rock climbing together and talk," Charlie said. "Mainly I listened to him. We would celebrate when he hadn't looked at pornography for a day or two—or even just for several hours. And we would remind ourselves of God's grace that would be there when tomorrow's temptation came."

As I listened to Charlie describe his relationship with his friend, I heard what seemed to me at that time to be a rare compassion, understanding, and respect in his voice. It was several weeks later when, after dinner at an Indian restaurant downtown, I decided to take a risk and trust that this same sensitivity might be there for me. "Could we talk about something before we head home?" I blurted out, feeling only a little relief from the sense of dread that had been gnawing in my gut as we had chatted over dinner.

"Sure," Charlie said. Was he wondering why my voice was shaking? He pulled off the road, parked his

Ford Explorer in our church's lot, and turned off the engine. It was October, and I shivered as the cool fall air found its way into the vehicle.

"There's something I'd like you to know about me," I began weakly. I told him that I knew I was gay. I had known since puberty, or soon after, and had probably experienced some foretastes of my sexual orientation even as a child. I told him I had prayed for healing. I said I just wanted Christian friends—including friends my age, peers—who would be there for me, who would help me figure out how to live with a tension and confusion that at the time seemed overwhelming.

When I finished, Charlie was quiet. "Did you want to say anything else?" he asked. I shook my head, wondering if I had said too much. "Wes, I just want you to know that I don't think this is weird."

"But it *is* weird!" I exclaimed.

"No, that's not what I mean," Charlie said, still quiet. "I mean, I don't want you to feel like this is weird for me to hear. I always feel overwhelmed when people share things like this with me, like, Why me? What did I do to deserve to listen to a—like, a sacred trust, like this, you know?" We kept talking until we got too cold; then Charlie started the engine again, we prayed, and he drove me back to my apartment.

The rest of my time in Minneapolis was a mixture of intense, dogged affliction and loving pastoral care and nurture from Charlie and a few others—pastors, older married friends, other singles—whom I told about my sexuality. I began to learn to wrestle with my homosexuality *in community* over many late-night cups of coffee and in tear-soaked, face-on-the-floor times of prayer with members of my church.

"These years at Daybreak have not been easy," wrote Henri Nouwen of his life at the L'Arche home for disabled persons. "There has been much inner struggle, and there has been mental, emotional, and spiritual pain. Nothing, absolutely nothing, had about it the quality of having arrived."[4] I feel similarly about my time in Minneapolis. When I moved away after two years, I knew my wrestling wasn't over. But I knew also that something good, something decisive, had happened to me. No longer was I simply struggling; I was learning to *struggle well,* with others, in the presence of God.

***

I have found two biblical images to be especially apt descriptions of my life as a homosexual Christian. Both are from Paul's letters. The first is found in 1 Corinthians 6:9–11. "Do you not know that the unrighteous will not inherit the kingdom of God?" Paul asks and then gives a list of habitual sins that are evidence that God's reign has not yet conquered the rebellion in all human hearts: "Do not be deceived: neither the sexually immoral, nor idolaters, nor adulterers, nor men who practice homosexuality, nor thieves, nor the greedy, nor drunkards, nor revilers, nor swindlers will inherit the kingdom of God." Paul paints a bleak picture, not least for those who feel a stinging indictment at his mention of homosexuality. But the picture is not finished. "And such were some of you," Paul says, with an emphasis on how things have changed: "such *were* some of you"— *formerly* — *in the past.* "You were washed, you were sanctified, you were justified in the name of the Lord Jesus Christ and by the Spirit of our God." There were some of you in the Corinthian church, Paul says, who were stained by the sin of homosexual practice. But you have been made clean, he continues, probably referring to the Corinthians' water baptism in the name of the Father, Son, and Holy Spirit, the action that symbolized their spiritual cleansing and incorporated them into the fellowship of the church. With this initiatory sign of faith, the Corinthians were scrubbed clean from the dirt of old habits, forgiven, and made part of the community of believers. "You were *washed.*"

I know that whatever the complex origins of my own homosexuality are, there *have* been conscious choices I've made to indulge—and therefore to intensify, probably—my homoerotic inclinations. As I look back over the course of my life, I regret the nights I have given in to temptations to lust that pulsed like hot, itching sores in my mind. And so I cling to this image— *washed. I* am washed, sanctified, justified through the work of Jesus Christ and the Holy Spirit. Whenever I look back on my baptism, I can remember that God has cleansed the stains of homo-sexual sin from the crevasses of my mind, heart, and body and included me in his family, the church, where I can find support, comfort, and provocation toward Christian maturity.

The second image that describes my struggle comes from Romans 8:23–25. Along with the fallen inanimate creation, "we ourselves, who have the firstfruits of the Spirit, groan inwardly as we wait eagerly for adoption as sons, the redemption of our bodies." Paul pictures Christian believers as having a "down payment"—the Holy Spirit—on their future inheritance. But indwelt by the Spirit, we not only feel happiness at the pledge but also a gut-wrenching hunger for its consummation. Like mothers experiencing labor pains, we can only *wait.* "For," Paul continues, "in this hope [of our future bodily redemption] we were saved. Now hope that is seen is not hope. For who hopes for what he sees? But if we hope for what we do not see, we wait for it with patience."

So much of my life as a homosexual Christian, as I will try to describe in the following chapters, has simply been learning how to *wait,* to be patient, to endure, to bear up under an unwelcome burden for the long haul. Taped onto my desk where I write is a small sheet of paper with a quote from the German poet Rainer Maria Rilke: "Be patient toward all that is unsolved in your heart."[5] Having patience with your own weaknesses is, I think, something of what

Paul was commending when he described the tension of living on this side of wholeness. When God acts climactically to reclaim the world and raise our dead bodies from the grave, there will be no more homosexuality. But until then, we hope for what we do not see.

Washed and waiting. That is my life—my *identity* as one who is forgiven and spiritually cleansed and my *struggle* as one who perseveres with a frustrating thorn in the flesh, looking forward to what God has promised to do. That is what this book is all about.

CHAPTER 1

A STORY-SHAPED LIFE

When I was growing up in a Christian home and later attending a Christian college, it didn't take long for me to discover that the Christian church has a rather unpopular position on homosexuality. Throughout the centuries, I found, the church has believed and taught that homosexual behavior is contrary to God's desire for human life. And in recent years, while considering what we now know of some persons having a virtually unchangeable "homosexual orientation," most of the church—Catholic, Orthodox, and Protestant—has continued to claim that homosexual practice is out of step with God's will. Acting on homosexual feelings and desires is contrary to God's design for human flourishing.[1]

Christians initially arrived at this position through reading the Bible, and the same holds true of the church today. The Old Testament book of Genesis (chapters 1–3), together with Jesus' teaching on divorce (Matthew 19:3–9; Mark 10:6–8), presents marriage between one man and one woman as the God-given context for human sexual expression and thus, in principle, rules out homosexual practice.

When Israel's law comes to explicitly discuss the issue of sexual intercourse between two males, it pronounces it beyond the pale: "You shall not lie with a male as with a woman; it is an abomination" (Leviticus 18:22).

In the one place where Genesis mentions same-sex eroticism, it presents it as an egregious example of the moral corruption into which the cities of Sodom and Gomorrah descended. When a pair of angels come to visit Abraham's nephew Lot at his home in Sodom, a rowdy gang of men mistakenly assume the visitors are human males, and they demand that Lot permit them to have sex with the angels (Genesis 19:1–11).

The founding documents of Christianity, the New Testament, do not deviate from the negative evaluation of homosexual behavior found in the Old Testament. The Gospels record Jesus' teaching that marriage consists of a covenant union between one man and one woman, in fulfillment of God's original creative design. The early church in Jerusalem taught the same thing, and their apostles and elders wrote a letter to the church in Antioch urging them to live according to the dictates of Leviticus 18—"Abstain ... from sexual immorality," they said (Acts 15:20, 29)—implying that the Old Testament's rule against homosexual intercourse was still in force even after the coming of Jesus and the Holy Spirit.

Paul, following the lead of his Jewish upbringing and of the nascent Christian communities through which he traveled, depicted homosexual unions as outside the bounds of God's desires for his new humanity, the church. Men who practice homosexuality will not inherit the kingdom of God, he warned the

Corinthians starkly (1 Corinthians 6:9, 10; see 1 Timothy 1:8–11). And in one of his greatest letters, the epistle to the Romans, he chose homosexual activity as a graphic illustration of Gentile idolatry and unbelief (1:18–32).

On the basis of texts such as these, the Christian church has consistently and repeatedly said no to homosexual practice. For example, in the 1986 Vatican Letter on Homosexuality, the Roman Catholic Church expressed it this way:

> It is only in the marital relationship [between a man and a woman] that the use of the sexual faculty can be morally good. A person engaging in homosexual behavior therefore acts immorally.

> To choose someone of the same sex for one's sexual activity is to annul the rich symbolism and meaning, not to mention the goals, of the Creator's sexual design.... When [homosexual persons] engage in homosexual activity they confirm within themselves a disordered sexual inclination....

> As in every moral disorder, homosexual activity prevents one's own fulfillment and happiness by acting contrary to the creative wisdom of God.[2]

One evangelical church I attended for several years expressed a similar point of view in a position paper:

> We believe that heterosexuality is God's revealed will for humankind and that, since God is loving, a chaste and faithful expression of this

orientation (whether in singleness or in marriage) is the ideal to which God calls all people.

We believe that a homosexual orientation is a result of the fall of humanity into a sinful condition that pervades every person. Whatever biological or familial roots of homosexuality may be discovered, we do not believe that these would sanction or excuse homosexual behavior, though they would deepen our compassion and patience for those who are struggling to be free from sexual temptations.

We believe there is hope for the person with a homosexual orientation and that Jesus Christ offers a healing alternative in which the power of sin is broken and the person is freed to know and experience his or her true identity in Christ and in the fellowship of his church.

We believe that this freedom is attained through a process which includes recognizing homosexual behavior as sin [and] renouncing the practice of homosexual behavior.[3]

In other words, to those of us who know ourselves to be gay or lesbian persons and yet want to follow Christ and be a part of the community of faith and live out the gospel's demand for holiness—to those of us who are Christians, members of Christ's church, and are attracted to members of our own sex—the church says, "You must not act on your attractions."

***

I do not wish to offend you gentlemen, but the church too is like the chief. You must do so and so. You are not free to have an experience. A man must be faithful and meek and obedient, and he must obey the laws, whatever the laws may be.

Alan Paton, Cry, the Beloved Country

At times, though, for me and many others, the weight of the biblical witness and the church's traditional teaching against homosexual practice can seem rather unpersuasive. The list of Bible passages and the statements from the Vatican and other church leaders just don't seem compelling enough to keep gay and lesbian people from looking for sexual fulfillment in homosexual relationships. In fact, not only are they not compelling; these biblical texts and Christian pronouncements appear outdated, perhaps slightly cruel, and, in any case, not really workable or attainable.

Consider one reason for this. If it is really true that God is opposed to homosexual activity, then thousands of people who want to please God must be doomed to failure from the outset, since it can seem virtually impossible for anyone—let alone homosexual Christians who have no legitimate outlet for their sexual energies—to abstain completely all the time. Isn't God setting gay and lesbian Christians up for a fall from the get-go?

On a recent trip to visit some friends from college, I spent a Sunday in Center City, Philadelphia. After attending a morning worship ser-vice, I drove through "the Gayberhood," an area of town known, as its name suggests, for its gay-friendly establish-ments, barely three or four blocks from the traditional, conservative church I had just attended with my friends. The summer morning was turning into a bright, warm afternoon, and leaning my head out the window of the car, I could see rainbow flags fluttering from a red brick bookstore and hear music blaring from the open doors of several bars. What would need to happen, I wondered silently, for the people hanging out on this block to feel welcome in the church I just worshiped in? Would they have the impression that their lifestyle has compounded their guilt so much that God's grace and forgiveness are now out of reach? Would some of them feel hope sinking into the pits of their stomachs if they heard that being a Christian means they should give up expressing their homosexual feelings?

Suppose a gay or lesbian person *did* want to come to church, to try to practice some kind of spirituality, to attempt to find God—what then? I heard one struggling lesbian woman say once, "It's just too hard to try to be a lesbian and a Christian. There is no way I can keep from surrendering to temptation, which means that I'll never be able to live the life God wants me to live. I'll fall into lesbian behavior, and that will be the end of my attempt at practicing

Christian spirituality." It seems to many lesbian and gay people that God could not or would not forgive all homosexual acts. For this reason, the demands for purity seem impracticable.

There are other reasons the church's traditional no to homosexual practice doesn't seem compelling. One is that it simply seems out of character with the Christian message of love, grace, and abundant life. Occasionally it strikes me again how strange it is to talk about the gospel—Christianity's "good news"—*demanding* anything that would squelch my happiness, much less demanding abstinence from homosexual partnerships and homoerotic passions and activities. If the gospel really is full of hope and promise, surely it must endorse—or at least not oppose—-people entering into loving, erotically expressive same-sex relationships. How could the gospel be opposed to *love?*

Sometimes it seems that we gay and lesbian Christians are unfairly singled out by the church for especially harsh demands. After all, what other group in contemporary society does the church confront as directly and sharply as it does homosexual people? Heterosexuals are at least given the option of marriage and thus the possibility of having their sexual urges satisfied. For homosexual Christians, there is no such possibility. Unless our orientation is reversed—unless, in other words, we become heterosexual—gay and lesbian Christians are offered no hope that we will ever be able to fulfill our deepest sexual longings.

42

I once read the testimony of a gay Christian from the UK who said that he tried abstinence for a while and found it unworkable. He would have "good runs," successfully resisting temptation for weeks at a time, his hopes soaring, until the proverbial dam would break and he would find himself on the street looking for a one-night stand. Every time afterward he would feel miserable with guilt. His solution for this cycle of sin-guilt-repentance was to come out as a homosexual Christian and enter into a monogamous homosexual union.

Admittedly, I sympathize with this solution. On many late, lonely nights when my desires for gay sex seem overwhelming, I remember, "There's an easy way out of this frustration. I could find a gay partner and the long struggle of resisting temptation could be over." To say no over and over again to some of my deepest, strongest, most recurrent longings often seems, by turns, impossible and completely undesirable. If a gay Christian's sexual orientation is so fixed and ingrained that there seems to be little hope of changing it, should he or she really be expected to resist it for a lifetime?

Everything in our culture tells us that the scriptural witness and the church's no to homosexual practice are onerous, oppressive, stifling, perhaps even mildly sadistic. Being sexually active is the way to be most *alive* —to be fully, truly, beautifully human, a chorus of influential voices says. And if this is the case for heterosexual persons, surely it also holds true for those who are homosexual. If gay and lesbian persons deny themselves the pleasure of being sexually active, won't they end up living shriveled, shrunken lives? If the church requires gay and lesbian Christians to refrain from homosexual sex, won't that somehow dehumanize them?

I hear and read similar statements, transposed into a theological key, from Christians too. According to Genesis, "It is not good that the man should be alone" (2:18), these Christians remind us. What's more, Jesus castigated religious people who "tie up heavy burdens, hard to bear, and lay them on people's shoulders" (Matthew 23:4) and said that his own "yoke is easy, and [his] burden is light" (Matthew 11:30). Surely this means that no gay or lesbian believer should have to go through life without a partner who can satisfy his or her sexual desires. As a Christian friend once wrote to me, "If healing prayer and counseling don't 'work' and a heterosexual relationship is not viable, then well-intentioned, monogamous homosexual relationships ought to be respected by the church."

In short, for a variety of reasons, deciding to accept the Bible and the church's teaching against homosexual practice sometimes doesn't seem very easy.

***

Biblical commands are not arbitrary decrees but correspond to the way the world is and will be.

Richard Bauckham, God and the Crisis of Freedom

In the first several years after Jesus' resurrection, the earliest Christians became known for their countercultural lifestyle. Where the surrounding culture trumpeted materialistic values of accumulating wealth and comforts, the Christians sold their possessions and belongings and distributed the proceeds to the needy who were part of their fellowship (Acts 2:45). Where society scuttled prisoners and other undesirables off to murky dungeons, the Christians visited those who were so mistreated, often bringing food and warm clothing for these helpless outcasts (Hebrews 13:3). Where raucous revelry marked pagan social life—"orgies, drinking parties, and lawless idolatry," as one observer put it (1 Peter 4:3)—the early Christians were known for a weekly gathering they called a "love feast," in which they shared bread and wine that symbolized the body and blood of Jesus, whom they worshiped with hymns and prayers.

What was it that motivated a lifestyle so radically out of step with the prevailing norms and customs of the surrounding Greco-Roman culture? What gave rise to this early Christian ethic? As I go back through the New Testament, I sense that for the early Christians it was the story of the gospel—which they told and retold to each other through their preaching, through their breaking of bread and sharing of wine together—that functioned as their motivation. Becoming a Christian in those days meant "learning the story of Israel and of Jesus well enough to interpret and experience oneself and one's world in its terms."[4] The gospel was "a comprehensive scheme or story [the Christians] used to structure all dimensions of existence."[5] And this story fueled a radical, upside-down pattern of life.

The early Christians' countercultural allegiance to Christ—their "ethic"—doesn't "make sense apart from a set of theological convictions, symbolically and narratively presented in Scripture (for instance, the goodness of God's creation; the covenant with Israel; Christ's defeat of evil, sin and death; the inbreaking of the reign of God; and the empowering work of the Holy Spirit)," writes Scott Bader-Saye.[6] Viewed from the perspective of the culture, in other words, the early Christians' actions were crazy; but viewed from within the worldview of Israel's Scriptures and the gospel, their actions represented the only rational option.

Not only in the church but in many spheres of life, rules and demands can seem harsh and deadly if the rhyme or reason for the rules isn't easy to discern. A parent's warning ("Be home before 11:00 o'clock") or a professor's assignment ("Read and summarize this article") can be maddening if the child or student fails to see the bigger picture *within which* the rules make

46

some sense. For the early Christians, the story of God's work through his Son, Jesus, provided that bigger picture within which their strange, unnatural choices and actions made sense.

***

I can only answer the question "What am I to do?" if I can answer the prior question "Of what story or stories do I find myself a part?"

Alasdair MacIntyre, After Virtue

I have a friend who has dated several guys in the past and who is now living with a partner of the same sex. "I'm not a lesbian," she says. "I'm just in a lesbian relationship." As I've thought about my friend's relationship, it has struck me that my situation is exactly the reverse of hers: I'm gay, but I'm not in a homosexual relationship. That raises the question: *Why not?*

I have pondered—carefully, frequently, from this angle, then that—what it is that keeps me as a homosexual Christian from pursuing my sexual fulfillment. There is, after all, an obvious and easy solution for people like me who feel frustrated by their homosexuality: I could find a partner and learn to *express,* rather than repress, my homoerotic impulses. Didn't Paul himself say in one of his letters that "it is better to marry than to be aflame with passion" (1 Corinthians 7:9)? Given that option, there must be a reason someone would *voluntarily* remain in a state of frustration. Why do I choose to abstain?

On the surface, the Bible and the church's demand for homosexuals not to act on their desires can seem old-fashioned, life taking, oppressive. But could it be that if I place that demand into a larger story, then perhaps—just perhaps—it won't seem as irrational, harsh, and unattainable as it otherwise might? Could the Christian story of what God did for the world in Christ be the framework that makes the rules—"Don't go to bed with a partner of the same sex." "Don't seek to cultivate and nurture desires and fantasies of going to bed with a partner of the same sex"—make sense?

These questions have been the deciding factor in my choice to say no to my homosexual desires. In the end, what keeps me on the path I've chosen is not so much individual proof texts from Scripture or the sheer weight of the church's traditional teaching against homosexual practice. Instead, it is, I think, those texts and traditions and teachings *as I see them from within the true story of what God has done in Jesus Christ*— and the whole perspective on life and the world that flows from that story, as expressed definitively in Scripture. Like a piece from a jigsaw puzzle finally locked into its rightful place, the Bible and the church's no to homosexual behavior make sense to me—it has the ring of truth, as J.B. Phillips once said of the New Testament—when I look at it as one piece within the larger Christian narrative. I abstain from homo-sexual behavior because of the power of that scriptural story.

But how does this actually work out in practice? What is it about this Christian story that makes a strange, old-fashioned decree—"Don't have sex with a person of the same sex"—seem doable, even reasonable? How, specifically, does the nar-rative of God's accomplishment in Christ give me a context in which I can see that obedience to Scripture and the church makes sense?

In the first place, the Christian story promises *the forgiveness of sins* —including homosexual acts—to anyone who will receive it through Jesus' death and resurrection.

One of the most striking things about the New Testament's teaching on homosexuality is that, right on the heels of the passages that condemn homosexual activity, there are, without exception, resounding affirmations of God's extravagant mercy and redemption. God condemns homosex-ual behavior and amazingly, profligately, at great cost to himself, lavishes his love on homosexual persons.

Paul wrote to the Christians at Corinth, "Do you not know that the unrighteous will not inherit the kingdom of God? Do not be deceived: neither the sexually immoral, nor idolaters, nor adulterers, *nor men who practice homosexuality,* nor thieves, nor the greedy, nor drunkards, nor revilers, nor swindlers will inherit the kingdom of God" (1 Corinthians 6:9–10, italics added).

Immediately following this, however, Paul made a sweeping pronouncement of grace: "And such were some of you. But you were washed, you were sanctified, you were justified in the name of the Lord Jesus Christ and by the Spirit of our God" (v. 11). The New Testament rings with the good news that the "unrighteous" may be redeemed. Like the prodigal son welcomed home by his father in Jesus' parable, homosexual persons may be forgiven and set apart as God's treasured possession—no matter what they've done in the past.

First Timothy 1:8–11 has an indictment of homosexual behavior equally as stark as the one in 1 Corinthians:

> Now we know that the law is good, if one uses it lawfully, understanding this, that the law is not laid down for the just but for the lawless and disobedient, for the ungodly and sinners, for the unholy and profane, for those who strike their fathers and mothers, for murderers, the sexually immoral, *men who practice homosexuality,* enslavers, liars, perjurers, and whatever else is contrary to sound doctrine, in accordance with the glorious gospel of the blessed God with which I have been entrusted (italics added).

But, again, directly following this coldly condemning word comes a "trustworthy [saying] ...

deserving of full acceptance: Christ Jesus came into the world to save sinners" (v. 15), including all the types of sinners just mentioned.

In Paul's letter to the Romans, when the topic of same-sex erotic activity comes up, as it does almost immediately (1:18–32), Paul places it in the context of a grand narrative of God's recreating human beings—and, indeed, the whole cosmos—through Jesus Christ. Condemning homoerotic practice in sharp terms, Paul writes: "God gave [Gentile idolaters] up to dishonorable passions. For their women exchanged natural relations for those that are contrary to nature; and the men likewise gave up natural relations with women and were consumed with passion for one another" (1:26–27).

But this condemnation is situated within the most powerful explanation of the gospel ever written. "All [who] have sinned," Paul says barely two chapters later, "are justified by [God's] grace as a gift, through the redemption that is in Christ Jesus" (3:23–24). "God shows his love for us in that while we were still sinners, Christ died for us. Since, therefore, we have now been justified by his blood, much more shall we be saved by him from the wrath of God.... [So we] rejoice in God through our Lord Jesus Christ, through whom we have now received reconciliation" (5:8–9, 11). "Paul's references to homosexual conduct place it within the realm of sin and death, to which the cross is God's definitive answer," writes biblical scholar Richard Hays. "The judgment of Romans 1 against homosexual practices should never be read apart from the rest of the letter, with its message of grace and hope through the cross of Christ."[7]

Sometimes I think to myself, "If I've already given into homosexual desires this much in my lustful fantasizing, I've already ruined my track record. Shouldn't I just go all the way and chuck this whole abstinence thing? God doesn't want to forgive me yet again." But then I remember the gospel.

Christianity's good news provides—amply so—for the forgiveness of sins and the wiping away of guilt and the removal of any and all divine wrath through the death and resurrection of Jesus Christ from the dead. Seen in this light, the demand that we say no to our homosexual impulses need not seem impossible. If we have failed in the past, we can receive grace—a clean slate, a fresh start. If we fail today or tomorrow in our struggle to be faithful to God's commands, that, too, may be forgiven. Feeling that the guilt of past homosexual sins or present homosexual failures is beyond the scope of God's grace should never be a barrier preventing anyone from embracing the demands of the gospel. God has already anticipated our objection and extravagantly answered it with the mercy of the cross.

***

There is a second way in which the Christian story provides a context in which to make some sense of

52

the Bible's no to homosexual practice. The message of what God has done through Christ reminds me that *all* Christians, whatever their sexual orientation, to one degree or another experience the same frustration I do as God challenges, threatens, endangers, and transforms *all* of our natural desires and affections. Theologian Robert Jenson observes:

> After all is said and done, Scripture is brutally clear about homoerotic practice: it is a moral disaster for anyone, just as adultery is a crime for anyone.... Of course, every mandate of the law is harder on some, with their predilections, than on others with theirs. In this fallen world, that is always true of law, divine or human. Does God's law then mandate frustration for those unattracted or repelled by the opposite sex? I fear it does, just as, given the fall, each of us, with his or her predilections, will be blocked by God's law in some painful—perhaps deeply painful—way.[8]

Jenson's point came home to me on a recent trip to France. At the Musée d'Orsay in Paris, I saw a painting by the French realist Fernand Cormon (1845–1924) that hangs twenty-three feet long and thirteen feet high. From the first moment I glanced at the painting, I was captivated. The subject is a troupe of nearly a dozen ancient desert travelers, all of them in motion. Most are half dressed, the women, long past their prime, exposing sagging breasts. In the rear of the procession, there is a dog and a traveler who is carrying a carcass lashed to a pole over his shoulder. Everyone is dusty and dirty, and the background is a stark outcropping of sand and boulders. At the head of the troupe is the painting's focal point—an old man, bent but clearly muscled and weathered from toil and struggle. His gray-white hair is wild, his beard long and unkempt. When I first saw the painting, my eyes were drawn to his craggy body. Clearly he was a leader, bold and commanding, yet wizened and world-weary. As riveting as this painting was before I checked the label, it became even more so once I saw that *Caïn* was the title. *Cain.* This was a picture of the wilderness wandering of Cain—the result of the first murder and God's curse. Stunned, I stepped back to take in the painting again in light of this new understanding.

For me, viewing Cormon's *Caïn* was a reminder that the biblical God—the God of the gospel—is a dangerous God. Cain murders Abel, and God calls him to account: "Where is Abel your brother?" (Genesis 4:9). Although he tries to evade God's all-seeing gaze, to dodge the implicit accusation, God refuses to let Cain relinquish the dignity he has as a human person made in God's own image. God takes Cain seriously. He treats his actions as full of import by giving them consequences. He doesn't merely brush aside his sin; he responds by cursing him for his murderous rage but also by graciously providing for his continued survival (4:10–15). In a word, God *threatens* Cain's life—at least the life he knows and loves—with judgment and the possibility of merciful transformation.

Both the Old and New Testaments in the Bible are replete with such stories. Genesis tells of Jacob the patriarch wrestling with a man who turns out to be God's messenger intent on blessing Jacob—by *bruising* him. "I will not let you go unless you bless me," Jacob pants, hip out of joint, clinging to the one who represents the dangerous God he fears and longs for (32:22–32). Similarly, one of Peter's sermons recorded in the book of Acts climaxes with the affirmation that "God ... sent [his servant Jesus] to you first, to bless you," not in the usual way, to be sure—not by indulging people, like a cosmic Santa Claus—but "by turning every one of you from your wickedness" (3:26).

Sometimes when I ponder again what it means for me and others to live faithfully before God as homosexual Christians, I think of Cormon's painting and these biblical reminders that the God of the gospel is known by his threat to our going on with "business as usual." Far from being a tolerant grandfather rocking in his chair somewhere far away in the sky, God most often seems dangerous, demanding, and ruthless as he makes clear that he is taking our homoerotic feelings and actions with the utmost seriousness. Like Cain, we sometimes squirm as we relate to God. We experience him both as an unwanted presence reminding us that our thoughts, emotions, and choices have lasting consequences, as well as a radiant light transforming us gradually, painfully, into the creatures he wants us to be.

British theologian John Webster speaks of "the church facing the resistance of the gospel," meaning that if the gospel brings comfort, it also necessarily brings affliction.[9] The gospel *resists* the fallen inclinations of Christian believers. When we engage with God in Christ and take seriously the commands for purity that flow from the gospel, we always find our sinful dreams and desires challenged and confronted. When we homosexual Christians bring our sexuality before God, we begin or continue a long, costly process of having it transformed. From God's perspective, our homoerotic inclinations are like "the craving for salt of a person who is dying of thirst" (to borrow Frederick Buechner's fine phrase).[10] Yet when God begins to try to change the craving and give us the living water that will ultimately quench our thirst, we scream in pain, protesting that we were *made* for salt. The change hurts.

"Are homosexuals to be excluded from the community of faith?" asked one gay Christian in a letter to a friend. "Certainly not," he concluded. "But anyone who joins such a community should know that it is a place of transformation, of discipline, of learning, and not merely a place to be comforted or indulged."[11] Engaging with God and entering the transformative life of the church does not mean we get a kind of "free pass," an unconditional love that leaves us where we are. Instead, we get a fiercely demanding love, a divine love that will never let us escape from its purifying, renovating, and ultimately healing grip.

And this means that our pain—the pain of having our deeply ingrained inclinations and desires blocked and confronted by God's demand for purity in the gospel—far from being a sign of our *failure* to live the life God wants, may actually be the mark of our *faithfulness.* We groan in frustration *because* of our fidelity to the gospel's call. And though we may miss out in the short run on lives of personal fulfillment and sexual satisfaction, in the long run the cruelest thing that God could do would be to leave us alone with our desires, to spare us the affliction of his refining care.

"Not only does God in Christ take people as they are: He takes them in order to transform them into what He wants them to be," writes historian Andrew Walls.[12] In light of this, is it any surprise that we homosexual Christians must experience such a transformation along with the rest of the community of faith?

***

The Christian story proclaims that our bodies belong to God and have become members of the corporate, communal body of Christ. This is yet a third reason Scripture and the church's no to homosexual practice make sense to me.

From the first page of Genesis, the Bible rings with the truth that we are, before anything else, *creatures.* The prophet Jeremiah and Paul after him both used the metaphor of a potter and clay: God is the master artist, and we are his earthenware vessels: "Who are you, O man, to answer back to God?" Paul asks rhetorically. "Will what is molded say to its molder, 'Why have you made me like this?' Has the potter no right over the clay...?" (Romans 9:20, 21).

The gospel proclaims that we belong to God twice over—first because he created us, and second because he has redeemed us through the work of his Son. "For none of us lives to himself, and none of us dies to himself," states Paul epigrammatically. "If we live, we live to the Lord, and if we die, we die to the Lord. So, then, whether we live or whether we die, we are the Lord's. For to this end Christ died and lived again, that he might be Lord both of the dead and of the living" (Romans 14:7–9).

Though it sounds politically incorrect to modern ears, the gospel has always said that God may demand from us what he wants, since we do not belong to ourselves. Strictly speaking, we have no "inalienable rights." God reserves all rights for himself. And this extends even to the realm of our sexuality—what we humans do with our bodies. "The body is not meant for sexual immorality, but for the Lord," Paul counseled the Corinthians, adding, "and the Lord [is] for the body" (1 Corinthians 6:13). "You are not your own," he wrote, "for you were bought with a price. So glorify God in your body" (vv. 19–20).

But not only do our bodies belong to the Lord. In Paul's estimation, they belong to one another as well: "For as in one [physical] body we have many members, ... so we, though many, are one body in Christ, and individually members one of another" (Romans 12:4, 5). One would be hard-pressed to find a statement more drastically opposed to our popular notions of personal autonomy and democratic independence. New Testament scholar Richard Hays writes:

> Through baptism, Christians have entered a corporate whole whose health is at stake in the conduct of all its members. Sin is like an infection in the body; thus, moral action is not merely a matter of individual freedom and preference.... The New Testament never considers sexual conduct a matter of purely private concern between consenting adults. According to Paul, everything that we do as Christians, including our sexual practices, affects the whole body of Christ.[13]

From the gospel's point of view, then, there is no absolute right or unconditional guarantee of sexual fulfillment for Christian believers. And this is one more reason the Bible and the church's prohibitions of homoeroticism have seemed less and less surprising or arbitrary or unfair the more I've thought about them within the context of the gospel. If *all* Christians must surrender their bodies to God in Christ whenever they enter the fellowship of Christ's body, then it should come as no great shock that God might actually make demands of those Christians and their bodies—demands proving that God, and God alone, has authority over us.

***

Fourth, and finally, the Christian story commends long-suffering endurance as a participation in the sufferings of Christ. In light of this, my objection that abstaining from homosexual sex will be too difficult doesn't seem as strong or compelling as it once did.

While taking a German class in college, I learned that in some old Teutonic and Scandinavian religions and mythologies there is an ideal of the "fated warrior." This is the champion who heads into battle fully aware that doom awaits him at the end. "Defeat rather than victory is the mark of the true hero; the warrior goes out to meet his inevitable fate with open eyes."[14]

Since making this discovery, I have thought often that this idealized picture resonates profoundly with the Christian story. One of the hardest-to-swallow, most countercultural, counterintuitive implications of the gospel is that bearing up under a difficult burden with patient perseverance is a *good* thing. The gospel actually advocates this kind of endurance as a daily "dying" for and with Jesus. While those in the grip of Christ's love will never experience *ultimate* defeat, there is a profound sense in which we must face our struggles now knowing there may be no real relief this side of God's new creation. We may wrestle with a particular weakness all our lives. But the call remains: *Go into battle.* "There is much virtue in bearing up under a long, hard struggle," a friend of mine once told me, even if there is no apparent "victory" in the short run.

"Learning to weep, learning to keep vigil, learning to wait for the dawn. Perhaps this is what it means to be human," someone has mused.[15] Significantly, this kind of long-suffering endurance is not a special assignment the gospel only gives to gay and lesbian persons. Many believers of all stripes and backgrounds struggle with desires of various sorts that they must deny in order to remain faithful to the gospel's demands. Homosexual Christians who choose to remain celibate "must face the dilemma of a life without sexual fulfillment," wrote Francis Schaeffer in a letter to a friend. "We may cry with them concerning this, but we must not let the self-pity get too deep, because the unmarried girl who has strong sexual desires, and no one asks her to marry, has the same problem. In both cases this is surely a part of the abnormality of the fallen world."[16] Schaeffer's language and outlook may be a bit old-fashioned, but his point is entirely in keeping with the spirit of the gospel.

Once, when I was at a low point in my struggle with my homosexuality, I wrote to an older single friend. "How can I go on living with this frustration?" I asked, feeling desperate. My friend wrote back:

Your email speaks in some detail about the desire for marriage and intimacy. To not experience this relationship means living with unfulfilled desire. But I assure you, even if you have to live your whole life without the blessings of marriage and family, you are not alone. Many, many people are (and have been) in the same boat. I am forty-one years old, a virgin, and one who has NEVER experienced physical intimacy with another woman or man. Do I long for it? Sure. But God's grace is fully sufficient to accomplish his purposes in me. Furthermore, I'd suggest that living with unfulfilled desires is not the exception of the human experience but the rule. Even most of those who are married are, as Thoreau once said, "living lives of quiet regret." Maybe they married the wrong person or have the pain of suffering within marriage or feel trapped in their situations and are unable to fulfill a higher sense of calling. The list of unfulfilled desires goes on and on.

My friend went on to say that the gospel does not necessarily promise a rescue out of the pain of living with homosexual desires. Instead, it is a message about God's strange working in and through that pain—God's "alchemy of redemption," as Philip Yancey calls it.[17] "My power is made perfect *in*" —not in the absence of, but *in the midst*

62

of — *"weakness,"* the Lord said to Paul (2 Corinthians 12:9, italics added).

One of the ways I have received help in dealing with my particular struggle has been through reading about the unfulfilled desires of others and how they have dealt with them. Schaeffer mentioned the many heterosexuals who would like to marry but for whatever reason cannot find the right partner. Persons in that situation, if they are Christians, must struggle to subordinate their desires for sex to the gospel's demands for purity. They must choose, again and again, to forgo sexual fulfillment. And there are many others in similar situations.

At a time in my life when I was wrestling earnestly with self-denial, a friend of mine who knows my struggle well handed me a copy of Wendell Berry's novel *Jayber Crow.* [18] In it Berry tells the story of a gentle barber who sets up shop in the fictional town of Port William, Kentucky, during the Great Depression years. Soon after arriving, he catches the eye of a girl named Mattie Keith, several years his junior. "The brief, laughing look that she gave me made me feel extraordinarily seen, as if after that I might be visible in the dark," Jayber wistfully recalls.[19]

Years after this initial encounter, Mattie ends up marrying Troy Chatham, a worthless loafer who, as the novel progresses, dismantles bit by bit the beauty and delicate balance of the rich farmland he inherits from Mattie's folks. As Mattie's admiration for her husband gradually unravels, Jayber finds that his admiration for her has blossomed into love. It hit him with the force of revelation one day out of the blue.

"For a long time I did not know what to make of it," Jayber says later of the experience. "What business had an ineligible bachelor to be in love with a married woman?" Toward the end of the novel, Jayber weighs his options, tormented by the conflict between his feelings for Mattie and his honor and integrity. He cannot declare his affections, he decides. Rather, one day as he stands in the middle of the Kentucky woods he is so fond of, in a strange, solitary ceremony, he makes a vow, before God, that he will love and cherish Mattie as he would his wife, if he had one.

From time to time, he questioned his decision. "Is it *legal* to be married to somebody who is not married to you?" a voice in his head asked.

I said, "I guess it's legal to be married to any number of people as long as they don't know it."

"But there's not any comfort in that."

"No," I said. "No comfort." But I had to laugh.

I had not, you see, arrived at any place of rest. Maybe I had not solved a single problem or come any nearer to the peace which passeth all understanding. But I was changed.[20]

Jayber mused, "Sometimes I knew in all my mind and heart why I had done what I had done, and I welcomed the sacrifice. But there were times too when I lived in a desert and felt no joy and saw no

64

hope and could not remember my old feelings. Then I lived by faith alone, faith without hope."[21]

This was the price of faithfulness for Jayber Crow. He willingly accepted the pain of living without Mattie for the sake of a higher commitment. He chose not to tell Mattie of his love, not to sleep with her, in the slim confidence that such fidelity would one day make sense and be repaid somehow. The connections of Jayber's struggle to mine as a homosexual Christian are not hard to see.

Stories of imperfect faithfulness and perseverance like this one inspire me and give me hope. I am not alone as a homosexual Christian. I am not the only one who has chosen voluntarily to say no to impulses I believe are out of step with God's desires.

"If anyone would come after me," Jesus said, "let him deny himself and take up his cross daily and follow me" (Luke 9:23). With these words, Jesus issued the marching orders everyone who chooses to become a Christian must accept. Suffering like Jayber Crow's in his desire for a married woman or mine with my same-sex attraction—all of it, seen from the vantage point of faith, is obedience to Jesus' call for us to join him in his dying and self-denial.

The sorrow and suffering we experience as homosexual Christians is that of saying good-bye to any sure hope of satisfying our sexual cravings. In choosing fidelity to the gospel, we agree to bear up under this burden for as long as is necessary.

***

The Christian story proclaims that all the demands of Scripture are ultimately summons, calls, invitations—beckoning us to experience true, beautiful, and good humanness.

C.S. Lewis once faced the question: Won't pursuing Christian holiness make me naive, less worldly-wise, less experienced? If I follow the dictates of the gospel, I'll become a sheltered, backwoods bumpkin, unaware of and irrelevant to real human experience! To this objection, Lewis wrote:

> A silly idea is current that good people do not know what temptation means. This is an obvious lie. Only those who try to resist temptation know how strong it is.... A man who gives in to temptation after five minutes simply does not know what it would have been like an hour later. That is why bad people, in one sense know very little about badness. They have lived a sheltered life by always giving in.... Christ, because he was the only man who never yielded to temptation, is also the only man who knows to the full what temptation means—the only complete realist.[22]

I've spent a lot of time pondering this passage from Lewis. I've come to see more and more that it involves a reversal of perception, an alteration of values. Many might say that for me as a gay Christian to abstain from homosexual sex means that I'm

66

choosing to prudishly, pitiably shelter myself from the only life worth living. Lewis turns the tables on this kind of an objection, audaciously claiming that, no, in fact, it's the sexually active homosexual person who misses out.

But I've also come to see that a bold claim like Lewis's works only if we accept the New Testament's teaching that Jesus Christ is the measure of true humanity. "Behold the man!" cried Pilate at Jesus' trial, speaking better than he knew (John 19:5). As Karl Barth declared, "This man is *man.*" [23] Woven into the fabric of Christian theology is the insistence that Jesus Christ is the truest, most perfect, most glorious human being who has ever lived—and that those who want to experience true, full, rich humanness must become like him, must pattern their lives after Jesus' humanity (Romans 8:29; Ephesians 4:20–24; Colossians 3:1–17).

"Jesus is the model of the fulfilled human being," biblical scholar Walter Moberly writes. "The Gospels portray a compelling and attractive person, who engages seriously with people and is good company at a party. Yet all the evidence is that he lived as a sexual celibate."[24] It may come as a surprise in our age of personal gratification that Jesus never married and never had sex—with a woman or with a man. He never gave in to any lust. Although he experienced every human temptation (Hebrews 4:15), he never sinned sexually. And yet he was the truest, fullest human being who has ever lived. Indeed, *precisely because* he never sinned, he was truly, fully human. From the Bible's perspective, sin mars and stains humanity. But Jesus never felt that stain.

Does this mean that everyone who wants to share the true humanity of Jesus must be single and celibate? No. It does, however, shift the terms of our modern thinking about sexuality. It dislodges our assumption that having sex is necessary to be truly, fully alive. If Jesus abstained and if he is the measure of what counts as true humanity, then I may abstain too—and trust that, in so doing, I will not ultimately lose.

Moberly asks, "Are we willing to find our identity in Christ, and our appropriate lifestyle in faithfulness to him, rather than in the fashions of contemporary gay movements? And can we learn to recognize celibacy as a life-enhancing vocation of faithfulness to Christ?"[25] Imitating Jesus; conforming my thoughts, beliefs, desires, and hopes to his; sharing his life; embracing his gospel's no to homosexual practice—I become *more* fully alive, not less. According to the Christian story, true Christlike holiness is the same thing as true humanness. To renounce homosexual behavior is to say yes to full, rich, abundant life.

***

There was a time in my struggle with homosexuality when I felt that the world was caving in on me. I

68

had been living in Minneapolis for only a few months, and I felt burdened—physically so, at times—by loneliness, confusion, and fear. During a brief visit back to Wheaton, Illinois, where I had graduated from college, I arranged to meet with my good friend Chris, and on a cold winter afternoon, I told him how I was feeling and asked for his help.

Out of all the things Chris said to me in response that day, one sticks out. With compassion in his voice, he said: "Origen, the great Christian theologian of the early church, believed that our souls existed with God before we were born. What if he were right? I don't believe he was, but imagine for a moment if he were. Imagine yourself standing in the presence of God, looking down from heaven on the earthly life you're about to be born into, and God says to you, 'Wes, I'm going to send you into the world for sixty or seventy or eighty years. It will be hard. In fact, it will be more painful and confusing and distressing than you can now imagine. You will have a thorn in your flesh, a homosexual orientation that is the result of your entering a world that sin and death have broken, and you may wrestle with it all your life. But I will be with you. I will be watching every step you take, guiding you by my Spirit, supplying you with grace sufficient for each day. And at the end of your journey, you will see my face again, and the joy we share then will be born out of the agonies you faithfully endured by the power I gave you. And no one will take that joy—that solid resurrection joy, which, if you experienced it now, would crush you with its weight—away from you."

"Wesley," Chris said, looking me in the eye, "wouldn't you say yes to the journey if you had had that conversation with God?" I nodded, and Chris's grew stronger, his eyes flashing deep care and concern, "But you *have* had it, in a sense. God *is* the author of your story. He is watching, supplying you with his Spirit moment by moment. And he will raise your body from the dead to live with him and all the great company of the redeemed forever. And the joy you will have in that moment will be yours for all eternity. Can you endure knowing that? Can you keep walking the lonely road if you remember he's looking on and delights to help you persevere?"

Your struggle isn't a mindless, unobserved string of random disappointments, I heard Chris say that day. And faithfulness is never a gamble. It *will* be worth it. The joy then will be worth the struggle now. In the end, I think that is how I am learning to live faithfully as a homosexual Christian.

PART TWO INTERLUDE

THE BEAUTIFUL INCISION

THE BEAUTIFUL INCISION

I first heard the name Henri Nouwen when I was in high school. I knew only that he was a Catholic priest and a popular writer on Christian spirituality when I picked up an illustrated hardcover edition of his *The Return of the Prodigal Son* at my local public library.[1]

Ostensibly a meditation on Jesus' parable found in Luke 15, Nouwen's book is more than a simple Bible study; in it Nouwen explores his own relationship to God through the lens of Rembrandt van Rijn's seventeenth-century painting *The Prodigal Son.* (A Dutchman, Nouwen spoke often of the affinity he felt for the work of artists such as Van Gogh and Rembrandt, who were also from the Netherlands.)

Nouwen describes in the introduction to *The Return of the Prodigal Son* how he traveled to St. Petersburg, Russia, and stayed for hours at the Hermitage Museum, sitting in front of Rembrandt's masterpiece, taking in every detail and gradually coming to identify with each figure—the rebellious younger son, the dutiful older brother, and the compassion-filled and welcoming father. As a result, he was able to inhabit Jesus' parable more fully, and the story became for him a kind of arc he could use to trace his own spiritual journey.

When I read Nouwen's book for the first time, I was at the height of adolescence, insecure and full of questions and confusion. Growing up as the firstborn son in my family and attending a fundamentalist church, I had always played the part of the respectable, straitlaced role model. By the time I was sixteen, I had already expressed to my parents that I thought God might be calling me to full-time Christian ministry. At our church, people looked up to me as the one who led summer Bible studies and planned spiritual retreats for the youth group. Beneath the public persona, though, my interior life was a swirl of secret desires and fears. When I read Nouwen's portrait of himself as the older brother in Jesus' parable, I realized with a sense of mingled shock and relief that he was describing me:

> I often wonder if it is not especially the elder sons who want to live up to the expectations of their parents and be considered obedient and dutiful. They often want to please. They often fear being a disappointment to their parents. But they often also experience, quite early in life, a certain envy toward their younger brothers and sisters, who seem to be less concerned about pleasing and much freer in "doing their own thing." For me, this was certainly the case. And all my life I have harbored a strange curiosity for the disobedient life that I myself didn't dare to live, but which I saw being lived by many around me. I did all the proper things, mostly complying with the agendas set by the many parental figures in my life—teachers, spiritual directors, bishops, and

popes—but at the same time I often wondered why I didn't have the courage to "run away" as the younger son did....

I know, from my own life, how diligently I have tried to be good, acceptable, likable, and a worthy example for others. There was always the conscious effort to avoid the pitfalls of sin and the constant fear of giving in to temptation. But with all of that there came a seriousness, a moralistic intensity—and even a touch of fanaticism—that made it increasingly difficult to feel at home in my Father's house. I became less free, less spontaneous, less playful, and others came to see me more and more as a somewhat "heavy" person.[2]

Later in high school, I read more from Nouwen. I learned that although he had been a professor at both Yale and Harvard Divinity Schools, he had chosen at a crisis point in his life in 1986 to give up a prestigious teaching post and accept a call to serve as pastor in residence at L'Arche ("The Ark") Daybreak community, a home for persons with mental and physical disabilities, in Richmond Hill, Ontario. According to his biographer Michael Ford, Nouwen's decision to go to Daybreak "emerged from his own need for a community and for a home he had never found in the United States."[3]

Soon after Nouwen arrived at Daybreak, the community assigned him to care for a twenty-five-year-old named Adam Arnett, who suffered from epileptic seizures and could not speak or move without help. Nouwen shared a house with Adam and four other persons with disabilities. "Henri's job, like that of the other four assistants, was to live with the handicapped and carry out a range of duties, most of them alien to him," writes Ford.[4] Every day, Henri would wake Adam, dress him, bathe and shave him, make breakfast and help feed him, brush his teeth, assist him in getting into his wheelchair, and push him out of the house and down the road for the program Daybreak had scheduled for him, most of which consisted of therapeutic exercises.

"[Adam's heart], so transparent, reflected for me not only his person but also ... the heart of God," Nouwen wrote in a book about his relationship with Adam Arnett that I also read in high school, soon after finishing *The Return of the Prodigal Son.* "After my many years of studying, reflecting, and teaching theology, Adam came into my life, and by his life and his heart he announced to me and summarized all I had ever learned."[5] Through Adam, Nouwen felt that he learned "what it must be like for God to love us—spiritually uncoordinated, retarded, able to respond with what must seem to God like inarticulate grunts and groans."[6]

Nouwen's strange choice to leave the halls of the Ivy League academy and take on the slobbery, thankless job of caring for a "vegetable" like Adam made a profound impression on me when I read his account of it. In reaching out to Adam and finding his own life immeasurably enriched in the process, Nouwen proved the truth of Jesus' words: "Whoever would save his life will lose it, but whoever loses his life for my sake and the gospel's will save it" (Mark 8:35). "It is more blessed to give than to receive" (Acts 20:35).

For several years, all I knew about Nouwen was what I had read in these two books, *The Return of the Prodigal Son* and *Adam: God's Beloved.* Then one afternoon, I was in the library at Luther Seminary in St. Paul and noticed a new biography of Nouwen. I picked it up and started to read, still standing in the lobby near the "new arrivals" shelf. I remember vividly the shock and ache I felt in my stomach, as if from acrophobia or a sudden lurch, when I discovered that Henri Nouwen had been a celibate homosexual and, as a result, had wrestled intensely with loneliness, persistent cravings for affection and attention, immobilizing fears of rejection, and a restless desire to find a home where he could feel safe and cared for.

The author, Michael O'Laughlin, Nouwen's friend and student, wrote, "He had a deep need for love and acceptance that no relationship seemed to satisfy.... [He] even [feared] that friends would forget him or just disappear from his life."[7] As I read, I felt as if a perceptive counselor were diagnosing *my* condition. At the time, I was going through one of the most tension-filled periods of wrestling with homosexuality that I had experienced up to that point in my life. I felt isolated, tormented, and, worse, numb to whatever love, affection, and support my friends and church family were trying to extend to me. Realizing that Nouwen had struggled with the same longings and fears I was experiencing—and that he had struggled with them all his life—I felt simultaneously that a weight was lifted off my shoulders and that I had a long road still ahead of me with no end in sight.

I left the library that day determined to find out more about Nouwen's homosexuality and loneliness. That night I wrote the following in my journal:

What I read in Nouwen's biography is so shockingly accurate to the state of my heart so much of the time, it is almost painful to read it. It feels like it's publishing my heart for people who pick up that book to read. It expresses my "inconsolable secret." Many times I am seized with terrible doubts and fears—mostly about my friends' love for me, whether it is solid or not. I sometimes feel like I am on a roller-coaster ride from joy to turmoil. It seems that hardly a week goes by without at least one night of black despair. Like Nouwen's, my anxiety is most acute in my relationships with friends, particularly my closest ones. I, too, seem to have a very deep need for love and intimate communion and deep knowing of another person and exposing my heart and soul that no relationship seems to satisfy.

Nouwen wrote often about loneliness and his craving for affection, circling back to that theme in book after book, as if fingering a wound that never quite healed. On one trip to Latin America, for example, he jotted down the following in his journal:

What I am craving is not so much recognition, praise, or admiration as simple friendship. There may be some around me, but I cannot perceive or receive it. Within me lies a deadness that leaves me cold, tired, and rigid.... I attended a small workshop about the basic meaning of being a Christian, but little of what was said reached my heart. I realized that the only thing I really wanted was a handshake, an embrace, a kiss, or a smile; I received none. Finally, I fell asleep in the late afternoon to escape it all.[8]

Later, in another place, he wrote similarly:

Once, when I felt quite lonely, I asked a friend to go out with me. Although he replied that he didn't have time, I found him just a little later at a mutual friend's house where a party was going on. Seeing me, he said, "Welcome, join us, good to see you." But my anger was so great at not being told about the party that I couldn't stay. All of my inner complaints about not being accepted, liked, and loved surged up in me, and I left the room, slamming the door behind me. I was completely incapacitated—unable to receive and participate in the joy that was there. In an instant, the joy in that room had become a source of resentment.[9]

Nouwen's biographers describe how, ignoring international time zones, he would call friends around the world in the middle of the night and want to talk through—for the umpteenth time—his desperate fear of being alone and his longing for companionship and intimacy. Full of energy and passion, Nouwen would be soaring one moment—like the trapeze artists with whom he had a lifelong fascination—on an emotional high, waving his big hands in animated dinner discussions or lectures, only to crash into a depression in the privacy of his bedroom later. Strangely, he was haunted by a fear that no one would show up for his funeral.[10] Philip Yancey notes that in lectures and books on the spiritual life, Nouwen "would speak of the strength he gained from living in community, then drive to a friend's house, wake him up at two in the morning, and, sobbing, ask to be held."[11] Toward the end of his life, he even chose to undergo a form of therapy that involved him being physically embraced in a nonerotic context.[12]

As I have sifted through more articles and books about his life since that fateful day I spent at the library in St. Paul, I've come to see that Nouwen's struggle with loneliness, like mine, was deeply rooted in his homosexuality. Probably *because* he was gay, Henri Nouwen "longed for intimate relationships yet recoiled from them out of fear where they might lead." Yancey writes:

I have known several people in ministry who struggle with issues of sexual identity, knowing themselves to be gay and feeling trapped, with no acceptable way to admit it, let alone express it. I know of no more difficult path for a person of integrity to tread.... [Nouwen] was a celibate homosexual.... [With that knowledge] I go back through [his] writings and sense the deeper, unspoken agony that underlay what he wrote about rejection, about the wound of loneliness that never heals, about friendships that never satisfy.

Nouwen sought counseling from a center that ministered to homosexual men and women, and he listened as gay friends proposed several options. He could remain a celibate priest and "come out" as a gay man, which would at least release the secret he bore in anguish. He could declare himself, leave the priesthood, and seek a gay companion. Or he could remain a priest publicly and develop private gay relationships. Nouwen carefully weighed each course and rejected it. Any public confession of his identity would hurt his ministry, he feared. The last two options seemed impossible for one who had taken a vow of celibacy and who looked to the Bible and to Rome for guidance on sexual morality. Instead, he decided to keep living with the wound. Again and again, he decided.[13]

Nouwen was only six years old when he realized that he was attracted to members of his own sex.

During a stint at the Menninger Foundation in Topeka, Kansas, when he was in his early thirties, "he became more acutely aware of his homosexuality, which he saw as a disability, and it started to disturb him greatly."[14] The small circle of friends who knew his secret struggle sensed a "constant tension at the heart of Nouwen's personality between being a priest—and a famous one at that—and living with the painful knowledge of his sexuality, which he described as a handicap, another cross to bear."[15]

During the time he was teaching at Harvard in the early 1980s, Nouwen sought help at a Catholic center in New Orleans that offered counsel and support to gay and lesbian persons. While there, he met an iconographer who had painted an icon of Saint Francis for him the year before. Would it be possible, Nouwen asked, for the artist to make him a second icon? Nouwen wanted something that would aid him in his struggle to be faithful to the church's rule against homoerotic behavior, something "that would help him consecrate his homosexual emotions and feelings to Christ."

What resulted was a painting of "Christ with St. John the Evangelist, not in the characteristic poise of the Last Supper, where John reclines on Christ's chest, but one of Christ sitting on a throne while John approaches him virtually bowing." This icon, notes Ford, "became a metaphor for [Nouwen's] own struggle and liberation. He placed it opposite his bed so it was the first thing he saw in the morning and the last thing he saw at night." He now had "a visual aid enabling him constantly to say, 'This is what I offer to you, Lord. I offer you all of these feelings, all of this confusion, and I want to remain celibate.'"[16]

***

From the first time I picked up a copy of Nouwen's *The Return of the Prodigal Son* to the time I happened on his biography one afternoon in a seminary library in Minnesota, I have felt an uncanny affinity with Henri Nouwen. My parents still have an audio cassette recording of me preaching a sermon to a congregation of stuffed animals in my bedroom when I was six years old; Nouwen, at age five, played the part of a priest, saying Mass with a toy altar and specially made child-size vestments.[17] Growing up, I was the morally upright oldest child, ever dutiful to my parents and mindful of my church's expectations; Nouwen, too, fit the role of the faultless older brother, never stepping out of line, always aiming to please. I came to realize that, from an early age, I had had a homosexual orientation; Nouwen also, later in life, arrived at the point of acknowledging to a select few that he was gay and had been so since childhood.

Loneliness, as I will try to describe more fully in the next chapter, has been a defining struggle of my life. I think it is probably rooted, in a profound yet mysterious way, in my homosexuality. And in this, too, I sense an astonishing resemblance between my experience and Nouwen's.

In his classic work *The Wounded Healer,* Nouwen describes central, character-shaping desires he achingly experienced from the time he was very young until the day he died—desires for love, affection, companionship, permanent intimacy, life-giving community, a deep sense of belonging, a safe haven, a home. On the flip side, those desires, going unfulfilled, became wounds of rejection, alienation, and isolation. I know well these desires and wounds because, like Nouwen, I have lived with them. I *am now* living with them.

The wound of loneliness is like the Grand Canyon, Nouwen wrote, "a deep incision on the surface of our existence which has become an inexhaustible source of beauty and self-understanding."[18] With this statement Nouwen gave voice to the truth of the gospel that, under God's severe mercy, evil may be turned to good, pain and suffering may be redeemed and transformed, beauty may spring from ashes. "And we know that in all things God works for the good of those who love him, who have been called according to his purpose" (Romans 8:28 NIV). Through the incision—though not beautiful in and of itself—we may glimpse the beauty of God.

Nearly two thousand years ago, Good Friday gave way to Easter Sunday, and at the end of history, when Jesus appears, death will give way to resurrection on a cosmic scale and the old creation will be freed from its bondage to decay as the new is ushered in. On that day there will be no more loneliness. The wounds will be healed. I expect to stand with Henri Nouwen at the resurrection and marvel that neither of us is homosexual anymore, that we both—together with every other homosexual Christian—are whole and complete in the fellowship of the redeemed, finally at home with the Father.

CHAPTER 2

THE END OF LONELINESS

There are days when the knowledge that there will never be a place which I can call home, that there will never be a person with whom I shall be one flesh, seems more than I can bear, and if it wasn't for you, and a few—how few—like you, I don't think I could.

W.H. Auden, on his life as a homosexual Christian, in a letter to Elizabeth Mayer, 1943

Late in the evening on Easter Sunday, I slammed the car door shut, took a deep breath to try to calm the churning in my stomach (*Would I throw up?* I wondered), and stuck the keys in the ignition. I felt totally, eerily alone—isolated, unknown, unloved. This was the same way I had felt on what seemed like a million occasions before over the previous weeks and months.

I had just finished saying a "Minnesota good-bye"—a prolonged, chatty exit stretching from the den of the house to the front porch and lasting sometimes a half hour. There had been a party—my second to attend that day. After church in the morning, I had gone upstairs from my basement apartment to have dinner with a man who wore many hats for me. He was my landlord, my pastor, the supervisor of my internship at the church, and my friend. His family was there too—his wife and four kids—not to mention the other friends and acquaintances who had been invited or who had just dropped in because they knew at *this* house there was always warm hospitality and good food. In the middle of this communal feast, I had been fighting despair.

Midafternoon I had ducked out and driven three blocks over to an old Methodist church building that now housed a food pantry and homeless shelter. In addition to working there two days a week, I led a Bible study on Sunday afternoons for several women who stayed at the shelter and came early to get off the street and drink Folgers coffee. Agitated, I limped my way through my chosen text, prayed with the women, and jumped in the car after a hurried, distracted good-bye. I felt sick, trying to close my ears to the roaring of that old anxiety I'd felt too many times to count. I turned the car out of the shelter's back parking lot, coaxing my Honda past the potholes and gravelly cracks in the asphalt. I headed out of downtown Minneapolis and into the suburbs; the second Easter gathering I had been invited to was at a house several miles north.

When I got there, the party was slowing down. It had been going on since lunchtime. Now people were starting to leave, while those who stayed were forming small groups to start games of Scrabble and Boggle. I ate some leftover ham and watched, feeling worse by the minute. It felt as if I were on the outside of a set of giant glass doors. Looking in, I saw people on the other side relating to each other in life-giving ways—laughing, talking, sharing, lending one another their ears and hands. They were clumped in tiny circles of three and four or paired in couples for conversation. And no one seemed to notice me on the outside of the doors, staring in hungrily, wanting to be part of the relating but somehow unable to enter.

It was late and way past dark when I left my friends' house. How strange is it, I thought as I backed out of their driveway, that I just spent the whole day with people—some of whom I would count among my best friends in the world—at two Easter dinner parties and a Bible study, and I still feel so desperately, utterly, helplessly lonely? On the interstate heading back into the city, I prayed out loud in my car, "God, help me. *Please.* Let there be a breakthrough tonight. I need your healing and help."

When I finally got back to my apartment, I was shaking slightly, and a knot had formed in the pit of my stomach. I had worked myself into a mild state of panic—I felt like a poster child for OCD, a cross between Shakespeare's Hamlet and Anne Lamott—by the time I had changed out of my Easter Sunday clothes and into something more relaxing. I tried sitting on the bed, then on the sofa in the living room, but I couldn't get comfortable. Nauseous, I tried to pray and pull myself together. Finally, I picked up the phone and called a friend who has seen me in this state more times than I care to remember. "Hey, it's me," I said weakly and tried to put this inner turmoil into words once more for him. As we started to pray together on the phone, I broke down. The hot tears weren't really a relief; they were mainly a reminder of the buckets I had cried in the not-so-distant past, and they also raised the haunting question I was trying frantically to answer: How long will this last? How do you find relief from this kind of crushing loneliness? On Easter—Resurrection Day—I felt like I was in a grave.

***

The sense that in this universe we are treated as strangers, the longing to be acknowledged, to meet with some response, to bridge some chasm ... is part of our inconsolable secret.

C.S. Lewis, "The Weight of Glory"

All the people I love, I trust, I want to be around, all of them answer, with varying volume, "yes" to the following basic question: "Will you be there for me?" I've come to believe it's the question that houses all my other questions, fears, and longings.

Jeremy Clive Huggins

"All our lives we're searching for someone who will take us seriously. That's what it means to be human," a friend of mine once mused. Whether heterosexual or homosexual, people are wired, it seems, to pursue relationships of love and commitment. Maybe it's possible to be more specific: it seems that we long for the experience of *mutual desire.* We're on a quest to find a relationship in which we can want someone wholeheartedly and be wanted with the same intensity, in which there is a contrapuntal enhancement of desire. For many people, entering into this kind of relationship means stepping into a new world of radiant wonder and breathtaking beauty. The tingly, life-changing sense that *I am wanted!* and *I want another person in return!* makes everything look fresh and bright.

Rowan Williams, Archbishop of Canterbury, expresses it this way: "To desire my joy is to desire the joy of the one I desire: my search for enjoyment through the ... presence of another is a longing to be enjoyed.... [Romantic] partners 'admire' in each other 'the lineaments of gratified desire'. We are pleased because we are pleasing."[1] Relationships of love show both partners that they are lovable.

Music, poems, stories, and films say the same thing all the time. I remember sitting with a roommate in our apartment living room once, just after a girl he had been hoping to date turned him down. Her rejection had hit him pretty hard, and as he and I talked about it, he gestured toward his impressively large CD collection. "Just think—most of the songs on all these albums are either about wanting love, finding it, finding the end of loneliness, and it being the *greatest* thing in the world, or else they're about losing love, love being unrequited, and it being the *worst* thing in the world."

In Wendell Berry's novel *Hannah Coulter,* the title character describes how she first fell in love with Nathan, the man she eventually married. "To know you love somebody, and to feel his desire falling over you like a warm rain, touching you everywhere, is to have a kind of light," she reminisces from the vantage point of her old age.[2] "The knowledge of his desire and of myself as desirable and of my desire would come over me" without warning, she said.[3]

Hannah reflects:

> A woman doesn't learn she is beautiful by looking in a mirror ... She learns it so that she actually knows it from men. The way they look at her makes a sort of glimmer she walks in. That tells her. It changes the way she walks too.... It had been a longish while since I had thought of being beautiful, but Nathan's looks were reminding me that I was.[4]

Movies, too, express this deeply human longing for relationships of mutual desire. I still remember the first time I watched Zach Braff's *Garden State,* a powerful film that probes the depths of the ache for genuine love. Andrew Largeman is a young actor living in Hollywood making B-grade television shows. After his mother's death, Andrew, or "Large," returns home to New Jersey and meets Sam, a quirky, painfully blunt, astonishingly *alive* girl whom he gradually falls in love with. During the course of a long weekend, they share their secret fears and hungers with each other. "You know that point in your life when you realize the house you grew up in isn't really your home anymore?" Large asks Sam as they take an evening swim together. "All of a sudden, ... that idea of home is gone.... Maybe that's all family really is. A group of people who miss the same imaginary place."

According to Denis Haack, *Garden State* is a movie about young adults asking the question: In the end, will anyone be there, truly there, for me? Is there anyplace I can call home? Haack writes, "As love blossoms between Large and Sam, they feel the stirring of hope. 'Safe,' Large tells her, 'when I'm with you I feel safe—like I'm home.'"[5]

Toward the end of the film, the two sit together in the airport, minutes before Large's flight back to California is scheduled to depart. "You're not coming back, are you?" Sam asks, afraid it's over. "This doesn't happen often in your life, you know," Sam says, meaning "this kind of love." They had found it in each other. So why was he leaving? In the film's final scenes, Large sits frozen on the airplane, waiting for the departure from the gate. Why? he wonders. Abandoning his seat, he rushes off the plane seconds before takeoff to find Sam crying and bewildered at his sudden reappearance. He couldn't leave, he says. What could be more important than knowing and being with another human person through the good and the bad? "This is it," Large says. "This is life. And I'm in love with you, Samantha. I think that's the only thing I've ever really been sure of in my entire life." "I know [it hurts]," Sam acknowledges. "But that is life. If nothing else, that's life, you know? It's real. Sometimes it hurts. But, yeah, it's sorta all we have." Love—two people desiring one another and being desired—is life, according to *Garden State.* Love is all we have.

As Rowan Williams points out in his moving essay "The Body's Grace," the crucial question for the church to ponder in regard to its homosexual Christian members is: How can gay and lesbian believers come to know this kind of love, this awakening of joy and delight, which is the experience of mutual desire? Is there any legitimate way for homosexual Christians to fulfill their longing—a longing they share with virtually every other human person, both heterosexual and homosexual—the longing to be desired, to find themselves desirable, and to desire in return?

For reasons I described in chapter 1, I do not think the option of same-sex, erotically expressive partnerships is open to the homosexual person who wants to remain faithful to the gospel. Which leaves the gay or lesbian Christian with few options, it seems.

There is the possibility that a homosexual Christian—while remaining a homosexual—might choose to marry a person of the opposite sex. I have a friend who is gay, a Christian, and has been married for over three decades to a remarkable woman who knew from the beginning what she was getting into. My friend still experiences only same-sex attraction, but he has remained faithful to his wife. Somehow, they make their marriage work, despite not having sex. Such an arrangement is possible, and many gay and lesbian Christians have chosen this option.

But for those who go this route, the experience of mutual desire is often frustrated in a way that it would not be for most heterosexual Christians who marry other heterosexuals. The homoerotic impulses of one or both partners complicate matters, and desire may turn cold. A pastor friend once told me about a homosexual man he knew who got married and who, on the first night of his honeymoon, sat in a chair in a hotel room while his new bride sobbed on the bed. The man's desire for his bride's body was not what he had hoped, and instead of delighting in her desirability, the bride grieved her husband's sad realization.

I recently talked with a friend, Lisa, who, when she became a Christian, opted out of her lesbian lifestyle. Shortly thereafter, she met a fellow Christian, Stephen, who had left a promiscuous gay lifestyle after converting to Christianity and had just been diagnosed with AIDS. She fell in love with him, and he proposed marriage to her. But her pastor refused to marry them. "It would be like writing you a death sentence," he said to Lisa. Another pastor, however, agreed to perform the ceremony, and they were married.

When we talked, I said to Lisa, "Because of my own situation and my strong desires for a relationship, I'm very curious about your experience." I asked her about day-to-day life with Stephen. Then: "Can I ask you about sex? How did both of you satisfy your desires in your marriage?"

"It was awkward and difficult," Lisa told me candidly. "We didn't have sex very often," she admitted.

Stephen died from AIDS three years after being married to Lisa. "Just before he died, he told me—we had a very open, honest relationship with each other—'Lisa, I'm just now beginning to notice and be attracted to women's breasts.'"

Surely, in such a marriage, where one or both partners are gay and continue to struggle with homoerotic desires and temptations, there can be a kind of rupturing or handicapping of the mutual desire that ought to characterize marriage. In Lisa and Stephen's case, for example, there were emotional and physical desires on Stephen's part—unchanged longings from his hardwired homosexual orientation—that remained frustratingly present and unfulfilled as he tried to love Lisa well. These were desires she couldn't fully understand or satisfy, and thus Stephen experienced a sort of loneliness, as I'm sure Lisa did also, though in different ways.

96

Another option open to homosexual Christians who remain committed to the gospel is celibacy.[2][6] Those of us who live day in and day out with the disordered desires of a broken sexuality can opt to live as single people, fleeing from lust and fighting for purity of mind and body in the power of God's Spirit.

But with this option, perhaps even more so than with the first, it seems that the lack of the sort of relationship Hannah Coulter describes—a relationship of mutual desire—is even more searing. I once read the testimony of a homosexual Christian who found the celibacy option unbearable and, I think, eventually rejected it for a same-sex partnership of some kind. His words aptly express this keen sense of lack:

> I do not want to live life on my own.... Much of my struggle comes from the thought that my lack of someone to love and be loved by must be lifelong. Even though God gave me some very

---

2 Some Christians have gone further and spelled out what such a commitment to celibacy might involve. Rather than live alone, some celibate gay Christians may choose to join an "intentional Christian community" in which sexual purity could be practiced alongside other single and/or married Christians. Throughout much of Christian history, whenever Christians took on vocations of celibacy, they did so most often in community—in monastic orders, for example. Those committed to a life of sexual abstinence recognized that such a choice would best be undertaken not in isolation but with others and would be sustained by the rhythms of corporate worship and the mundane tasks of providing for one another's daily needs.

close and supportive friendships, as indeed he has in the past, those relationships would inevitably end. People would get married, or move house, or move back to their home country on the other side of the world—and I would be alone again.[7]

A friend of mine was at a Bible study not long ago where a pastor confessed similar longings:

I used to be married to a woman, but after ten years our marriage fell apart as I realized I was gay and that that wasn't going to change. I was pastoring at that time. Today I'm still pastoring, except now at a gay and lesbian congregation, because I've always felt called by God to serve in that capacity.

Like many of you I'm hoping to find someone I can share my life with. But it's hard and it's lonely. I know you can relate. I come home after work as late as I can into the evening, and then I stay up watching TV until eleven, twelve o'clock at night. You guys know what I'm talking about, right? I sit there in front of the television because I hate having to face an empty bed. I stay up and stay up until I'm so tired I know I'll be out as soon as my head hits the pillow. That way I won't have to lie there, awake and alone.

Sometimes I ask God about it. I say, "Lord, all my life I've served you. I've always pastored as you've called me to do. I got married because I was trying to do the right thing. I stayed with my wife for ten years, even though it felt like I was having sex with my sister. It felt so unnatural. And now after the divorce I'm still serving you in the ministry, and yet I have to come home every night to an empty apartment. Why, Lord? Haven't I tried to do what was right? Haven't I always sought to please you? After everything I've tried to do for you, why am I left with this loneliness, with nothing but an empty bed to come back to?"[8]

As I write this chapter, I am still single and celibate. I have never experienced—and have no way of knowing if I ever will—an intimate relationship with a woman whom I desire and who desires me. How many of those in my situation feel lost and adrift in the world, as I do so much of the time, without someone, a lifelong partner, who *wants* them, who longs and yearns for them?

At a time in my life when I was feeling especially lonely, I wrote the following email to a friend:

The love of God is better than any human love. Yes, that's true, but that doesn't change the fact that I feel—in the deepest parts of who I am—that I am wired for human love. I want to be married. And the longing isn't mainly for sex (since sex with a woman seems impossible at this point); it is mainly for the day-to-day, small kind of intimacy where you wake up next to a person you've pledged your life to, and then you brush your teeth together, you read a book in the same room without necessarily talking to each other, you share each other's small joys and heartaches. Do you know what I mean? One of my married friends told me she delights to wake up in the night and feel her husband's foot just a few inches from hers in their bed. It is the loss of that small kind of intimacy in my life that feels devastating. And, of course, this "small intimacy" is precious because it represents the "bigger intimacy" of the covenantal union of two lives. It is hard for me to think about living without this. Yes, I have dear friends—several who are so precious to me I truly do believe I would give my life for them. One of my closest is another single guy, about my age. But I know that things will change. He will move away or get married, and the kind of relationship we have will change. We will still be friends, hopefully, but it will not be like a marriage. And don't you think we're wired (Genesis 2!) to want the kind of companionship that can only come through marriage?

The homosexual Christian who chooses celibacy continually, to one degree or another, it seems to me, finds himself or herself longing for something relationally that remains tragically, tantalizingly just out of reach.

***

According to Rowan Williams, *God* desires us. "Grace, for the Christian believer," he writes, "is a transformation that depends in large part on knowing yourself to be seen in a certain way: as significant, as wanted."

The whole story of creation, incarnation and our incorporation into the fellowship of Christ's body tells us that God desires us.... We are created so that we may be caught up in [the self-giving love of the Trinity]; so that we may grow into the wholehearted love of God by learning that God loves us as God loves God.

The life of the Christian community has ... the task of teaching us this: so ordering our relations that human beings may see themselves as desired, as the occasion of joy.[9]

This is why, says Williams, sexual imagery occurs so often in the Bible as a kind of pointer to the transcendent reality of divine affection. Sexual desire—the flame of mutual longing between lovers—is a taste or analogy of what it must mean for God himself to yearn for a relationship with us.

I often wonder if coming to understand and believe that God does, indeed, desire us and that we are invited to return his desire might be the "remedy," in some ultimate sense, for the loneliness and craving for love that I and other homosexual Christians experience on a regular basis. Leafing through the Bible, I find dozens of indications that God loves his people in precisely the way that Williams describes, and I ask myself: Could this be the end of my quest?

In the middle of a judgment oracle against the tribe of Ephraim, for example, God suddenly interjects: "Is Ephraim my dear son? Is he my darling child? For as often as I speak against him, I do remember him still. Therefore my heart yearns for him; I will surely have mercy on him, declares the Lord" (Jeremiah 31:20). Elsewhere God cries out: "How can I give you up, O Ephraim? How can I hand you over, O Israel? ... My heart recoils within me; my compassion grows warm and tender. I will not execute my burning anger" (Hosea 11:8–9).

Through the Old Testament prophets, God portrays his love for Israel with the imagery of desire. "When I passed by you again and saw you," Ezekiel records God saying to Israel, "behold, you were at the age for love, and I spread the corner of my garment over you and covered your nakedness; I made a vow to you and entered into a covenant with you, declares the Lord God, and you became mine" (16:8). The Lord "will rejoice over you with gladness," Zephaniah assures God's covenant people; "he will quiet you by his love; he will exult over you with loud singing" (3:17).

The New Testament, too, depicts God's longing for his people—now clearly including Gentiles in addition to errant Israel. Jesus pictured God as a father scanning the horizon for even the faintest clue as to the whereabouts of his runaway son. "While [the son] was still a long way off, his father saw him and felt compassion, and ran and embraced him and kissed him" (Luke 15:20). Paul, meditating on such an extravagant display of grace, exclaimed:

> Blessed be the God and Father of our Lord Jesus Christ, who has blessed us in Christ with every spiritual blessing in the heavenly places, even as he chose us in him before the foundation of the world.... In love he predestined us for adoption ... the riches of his grace ... he lavished upon us.

Ephesians 1:3–4, 5, 7, 8

When the earliest Christians spoke of their experience of God's love, they described it as just that—an experience, with a profoundly emotional quality. "God's love has been poured into our hearts through the Holy Spirit," wrote Paul (Romans 5:5). "You have received the Spirit of adoption as sons, by whom we cry, 'Abba! Father!' The Spirit himself bears witness with our spirit that we are children of God" (8:15–16). "Though you have not seen him," another early Christian wrote to fellow believers, "you love him. Though you do not now see him, you believe in him and rejoice with joy that is inexpressible and filled with glory" (1 Peter 1:8).

In some profound sense, this love of God—expressed in his yearning and blessing and experienced in our hearts—must spell the end of longing and loneliness for the homosexual Christian. If there is a "remedy" for loneliness, surely this must be it. In the solitude of our celibacy, God's *desiring* us, God's wanting *us,* is enough. The love of God is more valuable than any human relationship.

And yet we ache. The desire of God is sufficient to heal the ache, but still we pine, and wonder.

***

When I was in college, I had lunch with a wonderfully eccentric history professor who dressed like Indiana Jones, leather jacket and all. Prior to his current profession, he had been a pastoral counselor and had talked with his fair share of gay and lesbian people. In the college dining commons, I described for him the case study of a counseling session I had just read. It was about a Christian woman who had wrestled with lesbian desires for most of her life and had finally sought help. The counselor whom she talked with had written about his experience of trying to help, and I had found in his write-up an especially clear statement of God's desire and yearning affection. Rather than looking to other women to satisfy your craving for affection, the counselor had told the woman, you should redirect your gaze to Jesus, whose love is better than any other. Allow Christ to fill the void. Don't try to alter your basic desire for love (an impossible task), he had said, but just change the

104

object of your longing. Shift your affection from women to Christ.

"What do you think of this advice?" I asked the professor. His answer surprised me.

"It sounds too spiritual," the professor said bluntly, between bites of tuna melt. "It seems as if the counselor told the woman to replace 'lesbian love' with '-Jesus love.' But doesn't that downplay the differences between these two loves?"

I nodded interestedly, and he continued: "In her desire for other women, the counselee wanted human relationship. She wanted to know and touch and see and be involved with another human person, whose facial expressions she could read and whose embrace she could rest in. But the counselor suggested she look to Jesus, who *is* human, yes, but who relates to other humans through his Spirit now that he no longer walks the earth. The lesbian woman could not touch Jesus. She could not look into his eyes and see his face. Nor would it be appropriate, if she could see him, for her to gaze into his eyes in that way."

"So what *should* she have done?" I wondered out loud. "Where *should* she have looked for the affection she wanted?"

"I think we need a more robust understanding of how necessary human community is," the professor mused in response. "It's no use trying to be more spiritual than God, you know! God is the one who created humans to want and need relationships, to crave human companionship, to want to be desired by other humans. God doesn't want anyone to try to redirect their desire for community to himself. God is spirit. Instead, I think God wants people to experience his love through their experience of human community—specifically, the church. God created us physical-spiritual beings with deep longings for intimacy with other physical-spiritual beings. We're not meant to replace these longings with anything. We're meant to sanctify them."

"So what would you have said to this woman?" I asked.

"Well," he paused. "I might have said something like this if I were counseling her: 'The problem with your lesbian desires is not that you're desperately craving human love (though we must not overlook even here the deceptive possibility of idolatry). The problem is that your good desire for human love is bent, broken—like all human desires to one degree or another. You need to be re-socialized into the human community of the church. Your desire for sexual relationships with other women needs to be transformed, so that nonsexual relationships with men and women in the body of Christ in the fellowship of the Holy Spirit become life-giving to you."

I left the lunch table that day with a new paradigm, and in the following months I found that Scripture seemed to be pointing me in the direction the professor had indicated.

When Peter complained to Jesus once that he had left many human relationships to follow him, Jesus minced no words in his rebuke:

"Truly, I say to you, there is no one who has left house or brothers or sisters or mother or father or children or lands [and could we add *homosexual partners?*] for my sake and for the gospel, who will not receive a hundredfold now in this time, houses and brothers and sisters and mothers and children and lands, with persecutions, and in the age to come eternal life."

Mark 10:29–30

Jesus was referring to the community of his followers who would, after his resurrection, become known as "the church." Those who must sever their most cherished ties in order to follow Jesus—or those who must give up creating those ties in the first place—are not ultimately giving up human companionship. They are trading what seems to be the only satisfying relationships they have or could have for ones that will prove to be at once more painful (because of all the myriad effects of sin) and most life giving.

One of the most surprising discoveries I made in the weeks that followed my lunch with the eccentric history professor is that the New Testament views *the church* —rather than marriage—as the primary place where human love is best expressed and experienced. In the Old Testament, marriage was viewed as the solution to loneliness (Genesis 2:18, 24). Now, however, in the New, "the answer to loneliness is not marriage, but rather the new-creational community that God is calling into being in Christ, the church marked by mutual love, as it is led by the Spirit of Christ."[10]

Perhaps one of the main challenges of living faithfully before God as a gay Christian is to believe, really believe, that God in Christ can make up for our sacrifice of homosexual partnerships not simply with his own desire and yearning for us but with his desire and yearning mediated to us through the human faces and arms of those who are our fellow believers.

"We must call into question any notion that the supreme expression of human love is found in marriage," a friend once wrote in a letter to me.

The ancients did not contend this (consider Plato's *Symposium*). And neither does the Bible. The Old Testament suggests that there is love between men greater than that found in marriage (2 Samuel 1:26). But so does the New Testament. According to Jesus, there is no greater love than the sacrificial love of one friend for another (John 15:13). Is it not peculiar that in writing the greatest discourse on love found in the New Testament, Paul chooses to put it, not with his discussion of marriage in 1 Corinthians 7 (here love is not even mentioned), but in the context of spiritual gifts in 1 Corinthians 13! And even when agape love is discussed in the marital context of

Ephesians 5, it is *sacrificial love* that is the model for marital love—not the other way around. Marriage is a venue for expressing love, which in its purest form exists, first and foremost, outside of it. The greatest joys and experiences God has for us are not found in marriage, for if they were, surely God would not do away with marriage in heaven. But since he has already told us he is doing away with it, we, too, can realize that the greatest things God has to give us are not to be found in marriage at all.

I remember praying once with a friend about my loneliness and longing for love. When we had ended our prayers, he reached out his hand and squeezed my shoulder, as if to say, "I love you, and I won't let you go." With that gesture and hundreds of others like it that I have received from fellow Christians, I have sensed God's love in a way that perhaps I would not be able to in any other way. The remedy for loneliness—if there is such a thing this side of God's future—is to learn, over and over again, to do this: to feel God's keeping presence embodied in the human members of the community of faith, the church.

***

What if the church were full of people who were loving and safe, willing to walk alongside people who struggle? What if there were people in the church who kept confidences, who took the time to be Jesus to those who struggle with homosexuality? What if the church were what God intended it to be?

An anonymous Christian who struggles with
homosexuality

Admittedly, entrusting our souls to the fellowship of the church, being open about our struggles with homosexuality and our longings for love, can seem to make loneliness worse, not better.

A heterosexual friend of mine, unaware of my sexual orientation, told me once about his friendship with a twentysomething Christian who was coming out of an "active" gay lifestyle. "I'm trying to minister to this guy, to help him make this transition in his life, and he shows up to our one-on-one breakfast meeting one day with a bouquet of flowers for me," my friend said, incredulous and embarrassed. I winced inwardly at his story. How many times have I made my heterosexual friends—the ones who know about my being gay and want to encourage me—uncomfortable in similar ways? Asking questions like this, I recoil from intimate relationships, fearing the discomfort and uneasiness of the ones who, as I know in my saner moments, most want to encourage me.

As I recounted in an earlier chapter, I still vividly remember the first time I talked with a vocational counselor about my homosexuality. I had just graduated from college a couple of months earlier and was entering a two-year ministerial apprenticeship program at a church in Minneapolis. The counselor told me pointedly, "I would hate for you to get to the end of your two years with your fellow apprentices and feel like you haven't gone deep with any of them." Then, in a question that has haunted me ever since, he asked, "Do you find yourself holding other males at arm's length for fear that if you come to know them deeply and intimately, it will somehow be inappropriate or dangerous or uncomfortable?" Though I had never thought about it before, I found myself answering yes. My very longing for loving, affectionate, yet nonsexual, relationships with persons of the same sex had paradoxically led me to shrink back from those relationships.

Loneliness dogged my steps during the two years I spent in Minneapolis. I was deeply involved in my church. I taught classes there, went to prayer meetings, and spent hours in the homes of various members. I worked with the wonderfully affectionate and friendly staff of an evangelical Christian inner-city ministry to the urban poor. I got to know several people who to this day remain my closest friends. In those two years, I felt more loved than perhaps I ever had before. Yet the paradox is that the same two years were among the darkest I have experienced in my life so far. I felt more insecure and lonelier than I had ever felt before. In the words of Charles Dickens, "It was the best of times; it was the worst of times."

I have a friend named Bill who has counseled me a couple of times. For many years prior to his current ministry as a pastor, he served with his wife, Tricia, as a missionary in Central America. Bill's stories of dodging bullets (literally), exorcising demons, surviving sicknesses and natural disasters, sharing the gospel, and seeing people come to Christ are the stuff of the best edge-of-your-seat missionary biographies. He told me that when he and his wife returned to the States, their friends and supporting churches seemed to want to hear only about these larger-than-life experiences. "Tell us the good stuff," they said to Bill and Tricia. "No one wanted to hear what my wife and I felt was the mystery of our missionary career," Bill now says. "We loved our work, and at the same time we wished every day that God had never called us to do it. Our time on the field was the best time of our lives, and it was the worst time."

Experiencing loneliness, perhaps especially if you are a homosexual Christian, Bill says, is similar. Loneliness can make your life painfully contradictory. You can be on a roller-coaster high one day and in the depths of despair the next. Sometimes you can experience both on the same day. Sometimes in the same moment.

Bill has told me about his current experience of being in a small group at his church. "I've probably never been more intimate or bared more of my soul with any other group of people in my entire life, and yet I feel lonelier than I ever have in my life," he says

112

frankly. "I felt the same way when I first started my missionary work in Central America. The image that kept coming to my mind was of me standing outside a window, peering through the glass at a party going on inside. I wanted to be in the middle of the party, but no one saw me through the window."

Does God's keeping presence experienced through the human faces of the church ultimately spell the end of loneliness? Yes, I believe so, in some eventual sense. But on this side of the fullness of God's new creation, the ache remains. The loneliness has not yet come to an end.

A year before his death, after having written countless books on the spiritual life, after having lived for several years in the L'Arche Daybreak community and having found there the most profound experience of human community he had ever known, Henri Nouwen wrote in his journal about his "inner wound that is so easily touched and starts bleeding again.... I don't think this wound—this immense need for affection, and this immense fear of rejection—will ever go away."[11]

During my first year after college, I lived in a basement apartment with a roommate whom I never got to know well. Two friends whom I did know well and came to love, however, lived several blocks away in an apartment together. On many long, quiet, lonely nights in my apartment, I would imagine the fellowship, the brotherhood, the camaraderie, the laughs, the serious talks, the intense discussions, the inside jokes, the small intimacies that I was sure my friends were experiencing every night. Why was I only able to look through the window at the party on the inside? That year—and countless times since—I have pondered the question that haunts me still: Why do I so often feel agonizingly, desperately, hungrily *outside?*

Over and over again, I come to friends and ask, in a thousand direct and indirect ways, "Do you really love me? Are you really committed to me? Do you really like me? Do you desire a relationship with me?" I asked a close friend once if he would still love me after he gets married. "Will I still be able to call you in the middle of the night to talk and pray?" I wanted to know.

For some, even those who have immersed themselves in the life of the church—and certainly for me—no relationship seems to satisfy this yawning hunger to be known, to be loved, to be inside some nameless space that remains frustratingly, confusingly closed.

As a senior in college, I read an interview published in *Christianity Today* with Christian counselor Larry Crabb about his healthy, decades-long marriage. "Are there any continuing frustrations in your marriage?" the interviewer asked.

"There's something in me that's very needy, yearning, craving," Crabb replied. "I want [my wife] to be curious about me in ways she isn't always."[12]

A friend of mine, Tim, had recently gotten married, and several weeks after his honeymoon I called him and told him about this interview. "Do you ever feel like Larry Crabb?" I wanted to know, "or am I the only one?"

"You're not the only one," Tim answered. "When I get home from work, it's great. My wife is there to greet me, and she always asks about my day."

I sighed dramatically into the phone.

"But the problem," Tim went on, "is that then I'm wishing she'd ask *ten more questions!* I'm always wishing she were more curious about me. I'm always feeling like I want her to know me better." Finding the end of loneliness, it seems, is complicated.

For we homosexual Christians, committing ourselves to the church and looking for the presence of the risen Jesus in the human faces of our fellow believers, pursuing intimacy with this community, refusing to hold friends of the same sex at arm's length in the midst of our confusing loneliness, doesn't always—or even often—remove or lessen the loneliness; it merely changes the battleground. Instead of fighting loneliness alone in a car on an empty driveway or an apartment bedroom on Easter nights, we're on the phone with a fellow Christian. Instead of staring at a TV screen late into the night, we're at a church potluck, helping our married friends keep an eye on their kids. In the end, as the Indigo Girls lyric has it, "We're better off for all that we let in"—including all the pain we let into our lives when we open up our souls to the fellowship of the church. That pain is better than the pain of isolation.

***

Coping with loneliness as a homosexual Christian requires a profound theology of brokenness, I think. Alluding to Romans 8:23 ("We ourselves, who have the firstfruits of the Spirit, groan inwardly as we wait eagerly for adoption as sons, the redemption of our bodies"), Richard Hays sketches the outline of what such a theology might look like: homosexual Christians who battle constant loneliness are "summoned to a difficult, costly obedience, while 'groaning' for the 'redemption of our bodies' (Romans 8:23). Anyone who does not recognize this as a description of authentic Christian existence has never struggled seriously with the imperatives of the gospel, which challenge and frustrate our 'natural' impulses in countless ways."[13] I have come to realize my need to take the New Testament witness seriously that groaning and grief and feeling broken are legitimate ways for me to express my cross-bearing discipleship to Jesus. It's not as if groaning means I am somehow doing something wrong. Groaning is a sign of my fidelity.

The poet Hafiz counsels:

Don't
Surrender
Your loneliness so quickly.

116

Let it cut more
Deep.

Let it ferment and season you
As few human
Or even divine ingredients can.[14]

Or as Paul told the Corinthians, we must not lose heart. "For this slight momentary affliction is preparing for us an eternal weight of glory beyond all comparison" (2 Corinthians 4:16–17). Our hope is focused on God's glorious future, in the light of which the affliction we now carry—a disordered sexuality and the loneliness that goes with it—will appear slight and momentary. Elsewhere Paul put it like this: "I consider that the sufferings of this present time"—including the longings for affection and the fears of rejection that come with our broken, bent condition—"are not worth comparing with the glory that is to be revealed to us" (Romans 8:18).

Pondering this coming glory transforms a theology of brokenness into a theology of resurrection. C.S. Lewis saw clearly how Paul used the word *glory* to point to God's future in which we will at last receive "acceptance by God, response, acknowledgment, and welcome into the heart of things." What of my feeling of being on the wrong side of a giant set of glass doors? In God's future, Lewis says, the "door on which we have been knocking all our lives will open at last." He adds:

Apparently, then, our lifelong nostalgia, our longing to be reunited with something in the universe from which we now feel cut off, to be on the inside of some door which we have always seen from the outside, is no mere neurotic fancy, but the truest index of our real situation. And to be at last summoned inside would be both glory and honor beyond all our merits and also the healing of that old ache.[15]

But not only will we be summoned inside the circle of communion with God in Christ; we will embrace and be embraced by the renewed humanity whom he has made perfect in his presence. On the last day, "Humanity in the presence of God will know a community in which the fidelity of love which marriage makes possible will be extended beyond the limits of marriage."[16]

But until that day, we groan in faithful anticipation. We long for the end of longing, the end of our loneliness.

PART THREE POSTLUDE

"THOU ART LIGHTNING AND LOVE"

"THOU ART LIGHTNING AND LOVE"

Over a period of several years, I went on a search to find books that would describe my experience as a gay Christian (I wanted to know I wasn't alone) and help me know how to keep living it. Lining the Current Issues shelf of my local Christian bookstore were numerous paperbacks suggesting ways churches could stand up for traditional marriage in the public square and soundly refute the arguments of liberal gay rights activists, but these books seemed removed from my situation. Over in the Pastoral Counseling section were nearly as many volumes proposing various therapeutic regimens that just might "cure" those experiencing same-sex attraction, but these talked mostly about something—the "gay lifestyle"—which seemed distant and benignly irrelevant to me. The offerings at the Barnes & Noble across the street didn't give me much help either. Instead of proposing to rescue homosexual Christians by changing their orientation, the memoirs and volumes of pop psychology I found on the Self-Help shelves there promised to rescue homosexual Christians by showing them how to jettison their repressive morality and live out their true identity. In neither case did I find anyone writing as if they knew about the paradoxical, pain-filled journey I was on.

But then I found Gerard Manley Hopkins.

Hopkins (1844–1889) was an English convert to Roman Catholicism. After studying at Oxford, he became a Jesuit priest, moved to Ireland, and became one of the greatest poets in the history of British literature, influencing such greats as T.S. Eliot and W.H. Auden and changing the face of modern poetry.

What is less well known, but what many of his biographers acknowledge, is that Hopkins wrestled for decades with what today would be called homoerotic inclinations or same-sex attraction. As Frederick Buechner notes in his deeply moving book *Speak What We Feel, Not What We Ought to Say:*

> All his life he was troubled by the feelings stirred in him at the sight of male beauty. Temptation was everywhere, and in his diaries he takes frequent note of it—a glance from another man that lingered a fraction of a second too long, a beautiful boy in the choir at Magdalen, "looking with terrible attention at Maitland" or at students walking in Christ Church meadows, the charm of some street child seen from the hidden vantage of a shop door.[1]

During his undergraduate days at Oxford, Hopkins became friends with a fellow student named Robert Bridges, with whom he carried on an extensive correspondence throughout the brief span of his life. (Bridges eventually published Hopkins's poems after his death.) Bridges had a distant cousin named Digby Mackworth Dolben, who came to Oxford for a visit as a prospective student in 1865. Hopkins was twenty at the time, and Bridges introduced Dolben to him, hoping Hopkins could show him around Balliol College, where the younger Dolben wanted to become a student eventually. They spent only a few days together, touring Oxford, and never saw each other again, but as Buechner puts it, "In one sense or another Hopkins seems to have lost his heart" to Digby Dolben.[2]

For three years, Hopkins wrestled with intense desire for Dolben—as well as guilt over what he understood to be the shame involved in this desire. His diary records nights of remorseful fantasizing about his relationship with Dolben, his wild thoughts trailing on against the warnings of the priest who had heard his confession. The biographical details are sketchy, but it seems that at some point, Hopkins may have even attempted to communicate at least something of his feelings to Dolben. In any case, there is a point in Hopkins's life where there seems to have been a falling out between him and Dolben, and Hopkins heard nothing more from the young man he had grown so fond of. As he summed it up in a letter to Robert Bridges, "I have written letters without end to [Dolben] without a whiff of an answer."[3]

Soon word reached Hopkins that Digby Dolben, at nineteen years old, had died in a river trying to save a child from drowning, and Hopkins was left alone again—alone with God—to work out the seething tangle of his longings and desires. "Either he had never found the courage so much as to tell Dolben how he felt, or, if in some way he possibly did, he had all but destroyed their friendship in the process," writes Buechner.[4] To Hopkins, in the aftermath of Dolben's death, God soon felt as unreachable as Dolben had when Hopkins sent letter after letter in countless, fruitless attempts to make contact. In wrestling with his own unreturned affection, he felt a darkness descend, and a desperate streak of fear, depression, and loneliness runs through many of his poems.

In one of the sonnets he said was "written in blood," Hopkins pictures his prayers to God "like dead letters sent/To dearest him [Dolben?] that lives alas! away."[5] Gone, if he ever had it, was any kind of serene, childlike faith. Hopkins looked at human life and saw brokenness; the world is "bent," as he described it in one poem,[6] and man is born for the blight of death.[7]

Hopkins felt keenly his own personal share in the world's brokenness and death. "I wake and feel the fell of dark, not day," he wrote describing one of many sleepless nights. Then, addressing his own "heart":

> What hours, O what black hours we have spent
> This night! what sights you, heart, saw; ways
> you went!
> ...But where I say
> Hours I mean years, mean life....
> I am gall, I am heartburn.[8]

In another place, he paints a similarly bleak picture of his isolation and despair. "No worst, there is none," he says, meaning there is no darker place he can journey to, no state of mind more tortured or troubled. "Pitched past pitch of grief," Hopkins says of himself in a typically puzzling expression.[9] Bookish and morbidly introspective, he felt that his mind was a treacherous valley full of ledges that could give way at any moment, plunging him into black despair that others who had never experienced it might find easy to mock. But not Hopkins. He could not laugh it off or shrug his shoulders. He hung on to his sanity like a climber gripping a narrow crack in the rocks with his fingertips. If you can see through the difficult syntax, the window into Hopkins's soul that the following lines open is haunting:

> O the mind, mind has mountains; cliffs of fall
> Frightful, sheer, no-man-fathomed. Hold them
> cheap
> May who ne'er hung there. Nor does long our
> small
> Durance deal with that steep or deep.[10]

Near the heart of this despair for Hopkins were the struggles facing homosexual Christians that I have tried to describe in this book: the struggle to be faithful to the gospel's "terrible decree" that we must hold in check our strongest urges and not engage in homosexual activity; the struggle to *belong,* to find the end of loneliness; and the struggle with shame, with nagging feelings of being constantly displeasing to God.

As a Jesuit priest, Hopkins knew, like Henri Nouwen after him, that his homosexual feelings should not be indulged, that he could not remain pure and faithful as a Christian and at the same time enter into a homosexual relationship. And this realization—whether he understood it as a call to true and beautiful humanness, or whether it felt like a burden from a cosmic killjoy, we may never know—brought loneliness: "To seem the stranger lies my lot, my life/Among strangers. Father and mother dear,/Brothers and sisters are in Christ not near," Hopkins confessed.[11] It brought shame too. As Buechner expresses it, "Throughout [his] brief relationship [with Digby Dolben], Hopkins apparently had a sense of guilt about his feelings for him. He notes in his diary that it is dangerous to think about him, and if his name came up in conversation, he quickly backed away from it."[12]

For several years now, I have kept a book of Hopkins's poems near my bedside. What keeps me coming back to his poetry is, of course, the similarities between our life situations: he was a Christian, as I am; he wrestled with homoerotic attractions and inclinations, as I do; and he (apparently) longed for purity, experienced an unshakable loneliness, and yearned to hear the divine accolade that would unravel his shame and inferiority—all things that I feel and experience on a regular basis. But most of all, I keep coming back to Hopkins because in the midst of his struggle, he saw God and came to know the comfort of Christ and the Holy Spirit—and he wrote about this vision of God and experience of Christ in a way that continually refreshes, strengthens, and emboldens me for the journey toward wholeness.

Hopkins knew better than many that God isn't tame or safe. True, he is merciful, but his mercy has sharp edges. God judges sin and transforms sinners in a way that often feels as if it is ripping apart our deepest selves. Hopkins also knew that even on our loneliest roads, when the valleys are so shadowed that day feels like night, God is watching, rejoicing over every inch gained, gazing down as the Author who cares about every twist in *his* story.

One of the most moving stanzas Hopkins ever penned was an unconventional hymn of praise to the triune God who is fiery and shocking like a bolt of lightning in a stormy sky but who is also—at the same time—tender and nurturing like an infatuated Lover. Paradoxically, it is precisely *in* the fierce lightning— *in* his "dark descending"—that God's loving mercy is best seen:

Be adored among men,
God, three-numberèd form;
Wring thy rebel, dogged in den,

128

Man's malice, with wrecking and storm.
Beyond saying sweet, past telling of tongue,
Thou art lightning and love, I found it, a winter
  and warm;
Father and fondler of heart thou hast wrung;
Hast thy dark descending and most art merciful
  then.[13]

Gradually, Hopkins came to see that his battles with despair and darkness were somehow included in God's loving purposes. Although he addressed God as the "terrible" one who had laid "a lionlimb against me," scanning "with darksome devouring eyes my bruised bones," Hopkins moved to a point of confidence that God was indeed merciful in the very moments when he seemed most ruthless. Hopkins, "frantic to avoid thee and flee," as he says to God at one point, discerned a divine *purpose* behind his struggle. Why did he have to wrestle in the ways that he did?

That my chaff might fly; my grain lie, sheer and
  clear....

His heart "would ... cheer."

Cheer whom though? the hero whose
  heaven-handling flung me, foot trod
Me? or me that fought him? O which one? is it
  each one?

That night, that year
Of now done darkness I wretch lay wrestling with
   (my God!) my God.[14]

The "hero" Hopkins mentions here is God. The poet has finally come to understand that God's purifying work of separating the wheat from the chaff, of refining and sifting Hopkins's faith, is for God's own "cheer," God's pleasure—and Hopkins's. When it seems that no one is watching and Hopkins is alone, there *is* Someone there.

God, lover of souls, swaying considerate scales,
Complete thy creature dear O where it fails,
Being mighty a master, being a father and
   fond.[15]

Elsewhere, Hopkins pictures lonely souls like himself as the "interest" or inheritance of Christ. Christ

...eyes them, heart wants, care haunts, foot
   follows kind,
Their ransom, their rescue, and first, fast, last
   friend.[16]

To engage with God as a homosexual Christian, as Hopkins did, is to find God in Christ to be ever-present, always watching, with ruthless, relentless, transforming grace. And one day, beyond all hopes, that grace will accomplish the ultimate transforma-

130

tion—changing human beings with broken sexualities and a thousand other afflictions into shining, everlastingly alive children of the resurrection.

> In a flash, at a trumpet crash,
> I am all at once what Christ is, since he was what
> I am, and
> This Jack, joke, poor potsherd, patch, matchwood,
> immortal diamond,
> Is immortal diamond.[17]

CHAPTER 3

THE DIVINE ACCOLADE

To please God ... to be a real ingredient in the divine happiness ... to be loved by God, not merely pitied, but delighted in as an artist delights in his work or a father in a son—it seems impossible, a weight or burden of glory which our thoughts can hardly sustain. But so it is.

C.S. Lewis, "The Weight of Glory"

The tested genuineness of your faith—more precious than gold that perishes though it is tested by fire—[will] be found to result in praise and glory and honor at the revelation of Jesus Christ.

1 Peter 1:7

Not long ago I was at the wedding of two good friends. After the ceremony and dinner, the band at the reception started playing, and the men, removing their tuxedo jackets and blazers and taking the hands of the women next to them, began moving onto the dance floor. Some people continued eating dessert and sipping coffee, and I lingered with them, since I had come single and had never really learned to dance.

But one of my old college friends whom I had spent the last few minutes chatting with wasn't going to let me stay seated. "Come on," she said playfully, smiling in awareness of my awkward feeling. "Karis needs a dance partner!" She led me by the hand as we threaded our way through the beautiful round tables in the reception hall, now piled high with dirty dishes and empty wine bottles.

Karis was a girl I had known a little, never well, when we were in school together; now it was time to try to dance with her, I guessed, a bit nervous. "Karis, this is Wes," my friend introduced me. I felt even more awkward. I had forgotten how beautiful Karis was. Her light eyes were flashing as she smiled mischievously, and her black hair fell in loose curls just above her shoulders. She was wearing a dress with spaghetti straps that showed plenty of her lightly tanned neck and shoulders.

"I should warn you, I'm not great at this," I said after Karis had led me onto the dance floor. "No worries," she said, "I'll show you how it goes." "Put your right hand here," she instructed, reaching for my hand and placing it on the small of her back. Step by step, she tried to teach me as my mind wandered. We danced for a while, experimenting with different steps as the music changed.

Next to us, several feet away, was another couple. They were good— *really* good—dancers. Full of energy. They were laughing and moving in sync with the groove. I couldn't take my eyes off the guy. I started to feel dazed and a little queasy as Karis and I kept dancing. Finally, perhaps sensing my frustration, Karis suggested we take a break. I stepped off the dance floor, relieved—and very confused.

A couple of days later I explained to my friend Chris over breakfast what had happened. We danced, I said. I was with this beautiful girl. I was holding her hand and touching her back. Her dress was thin and showed every curve on her body, I said. I could feel her sweating through the dress, and, inches from her face, I could see every exquisite feature she had. "And, Chris," I said, " *I felt nothing.* No attraction. No awakening or arousal of any kind. No sexual desire whatsoever."

Chris nodded. He knows my situation backward and forward and wasn't fazed by what I was telling him.

"The worst of it," I continued, "is that while I wasn't attracted at all to this stunningly beautiful person who was my dance partner, I couldn't stop looking at the guy dancing several feet away from me. I *did* notice him. I noticed his *body,* his moves. Chris," I said, "I was attracted to this guy. All I could see and desire was another guy across the room while I'm dancing with this girl. This is so frustrating. This is what it means to be gay, and I would give anything to change it!"

The year before that breakfast, on a cold, gray, late-winter afternoon, I had told Chris about my homosexuality. He and I had been good friends for a while before that time, and I had needed sup-port—again—and decided it was a good time to share with him this part of my life that was causing me so much grief. We talked for hours that afternoon. I read to him excerpts from my journals, told him story after story about my journey, and asked a lot of questions about how to live as a Christian with these nearly overwhelming desires. He listened patiently, asked questions of his own, and pulled books off his shelf to read me things he thought might throw fresh light on the issue. He cried and prayed for me and in the end gave me one of the best hugs I've ever received.

That day I tried to explain to Chris the sense of brokenness, the shame of feeling "this is not the way it's supposed to be" with my body, my psyche, my sexuality. "Sometimes I feel that no matter what I do, I am displeasing to God," I said. "Even after a good day of battling for purity of mind and body, there is still the feeling, when I put my head down on the pillow at night to go to sleep, that something is seri-ously wrong with me, that something's askew. I feel in those moments that my homosexual orientation makes God disappointed or unhappy or even faintly upset with me. Of course, the really frustrating part is that I can't just turn off this orientation like a spigot. I can't choose not to be gay. Does that mean I'm locked into this feeling of being constantly unac-ceptable to God? Can I ever really please him?"

***

Henri Nouwen, as I've already mentioned, struggled long and hard with myriad insecurities as a homosexual Christian. One of them was this hunch that he was damaged goods, broken beyond mending, permanently locked into a pattern of desire that made him regularly, constantly unsatisfying to the One he most wanted to please. Michael O'Laughlin writes:

One component of Henri's psychological issues was a real sense of shame, a feeling that there was something wrong with him that he couldn't correct. The origins of these feelings are obscure, but there was one factor that certainly exacerbated his sense of unworthiness: Henri was a gay man, and he grew up in a time and place in which this could not be acknowledged.... Henri grew up believing that he was different from other people, and thinking that this difference was so terrible that it must be kept a secret.[1]

For Nouwen, one of the main questions in his struggle to live well before God as a homosexual Christian was how to deal with this sort of shame. It is also my question and, I suspect, the question of many others who share our condition. Can we gay and lesbian Christians who experience no change in our homoerotic desires live in the joyful assurance that our lives are satisfying to God? Can we who remain homosexually inclined actually please God?

I have talked to enough heterosexual Christians about their desires and attractions to know that many of them consider their sexuality to be a glorious gift, and rightly so. Because God designed human sexuality, it is part of his good creation; he has sanctified it through redemption and means for it to be celebrated and enjoyed in the context of monogamous marriage.

But married heterosexuals are, of course, able to identify moments when God's gift gets stained, marred by lust—sexual desire that is fixed on a man or woman other than their spouse. And singles, too, experience lust by entertaining erotic thoughts and feelings for potential partners or spouses.

Dallas Willard helpfully defines *lust* as "looking *to* desire"—looking at someone other than a spouse *in order to* indulge in sexual fantasies. "That is, we desire to desire. We indulge and cultivate desiring because we enjoy fantasizing about sex with the one seen. Desiring sex is the purpose for which we are looking."[2]

This purposeful looking—the "second glance"—is different, Willard says, from "looking *and* desiring." Looking *to* desire is intentional, willful. Looking *and* desiring is natural, reflexive, part of the experience of a God-designed and God-given desire for intimacy with someone of the opposite sex; it could happen at any time, in any place—as you drive down the road and see a billboard, as you place your order at a restaurant, as you browse the shelves at a bookstore.

When we only *think* of sex with someone we see, or simply find him or her attractive, that is not wrong, and certainly is not what Jesus calls "adultery in the heart." Merely to be *tempted* sexually requires that we think of sex with someone we are not married to, and that we desire the other person—usually, of course, someone we see. But temptation also is not wrong, though it should not be willfully entered.[3]

Looking *and* desiring, according to Willard, isn't sinful; it's what you choose to do with the desire that determines whether the first look will turn into cultivated lust.

"Heterosexual Christians know that if and when temptation comes and they begin to lust, at least they will be desiring someone of the opposite sex," I said to my friend Chris on that winter afternoon when we talked together. "It's true that even their lust isn't pleasing to God. But at least they're attracted to the sex God originally planned for human beings to be attracted to!" For me and other gay people, even when we're not willfully cultivating desire, we know that when attraction does come—most of the time, it could be as unlooked for and unwanted as it was for me that day on the dance floor at my friends' wedding reception—it will be attraction to someone of the same sex. And in those moments, it feels as though there is no desire that isn't lust, no attraction that isn't illicit. I never have the moment Dallas Willard describes as "looking *and* desiring" when I can thank God that he made me to be attracted to women. I have only a looking and desiring that causes me to groan, "God, help! I would love to say thanks for my sexuality, but I don't feel like I can. Every attraction I experience, before I ever get to intentional, willful, indulgent desire, seems bent, broken, misshapen. I think this grieves you, but I can't seem to help it."

For many homosexual Christians, this kind of shame is part of our daily lives. Theologian Robert Jenson calls homoerotic attraction a "grievous affliction" for those who experience it,[4] and part of the grief is in the feeling that we are perpetually, hopelessly unsatisfying to God.

***

One spring break during college, I flew to England to visit my friend Todd, who was a student at Cambridge University at the time, and his wife, Katie. One night in Todd and Katie's house, as Katie was upstairs putting their two kids to bed, Todd and I stood in the kitchen washing dishes together and talking.

Sometimes you can look back on your life and know that certain moments changed your perception of the world, your take on life, your experience of God. For me, that night was one of those times.

"Wes, I've got to tell you something," Todd said in the middle of our conversation, his hands dripping soapy water. "I've just reread C.S. Lewis's essay 'The Weight of Glory,' and I think I've realized something I've missed for years in my Christian life: The climax of our joy in God, our joy in our salvation, is going to be the moment when we finally see Jesus face-to-face, and he commends us, honors us, praises us for the lives we lived on earth." Todd paused for a moment, gauging my reaction, and went on: "Lewis saw this so clearly. I don't know why I never saw it before in his essay. But it's right there, plain as day."[5]

Todd was right. Most of "The Weight of Glory" essay (originally a sermon) is Lewis's elaboration of the moment when God will glorify his people. "It is promised ... that we shall have 'glory' ... fame with God, approval or (I might say) 'appreciation' by God," Lewis writes. "Nothing can eliminate from the parable the divine *accolade,* 'Well done, thou good and faithful servant.'"[6]

Lewis points to what in Scripture is called "the day of the Lord"—the last judgment, the great assize—as the time when God will give us this glory.

It is written that we shall "stand before" him, shall appear, shall be inspected. The promise of glory is the promise, almost incredible and only possible by the work of Christ, that some of us, that any of us who really chooses, shall actually survive that examination, shall find approval, shall please God. To please God ... to be a real ingredient in the divine happiness ... to be loved by God, not merely pitied, but delighted in as an artist delights in his work or a father in a son—it seems impossible, a weight or burden of glory which our thoughts can hardly sustain. But so it is.[7]

"Since reading Lewis, I've started to see this theme of glory and praise for us from God everywhere in the

Bible," Todd said to me that night in Cambridge. He stacked the last of the dripping dishes on the rack to dry, and we went into the living room. Opening a Bible, he pointed out text after text in the New Testament I had seen a hundred times before but had never really paid attention to.

"Therefore do not pronounce judgment before the time, before the Lord comes, who will bring to light the things now hidden in darkness and will disclose the purposes of the heart," Paul counseled the Corinthian Christians (1 Corinthians 4:5), and adds: "Then each one will receive his commendation from God." There it was, crystal clear.

"For it is not the one who commends himself who is approved, but *the one whom the Lord commends,*" Paul wrote to the same Christians (2 Corinthians 10:18, italics added).

To the Romans he wrote, "A Jew is one inwardly, and circumcision is a matter of the heart, by the Spirit, not by the letter. *His praise is not from man but from God*" (2:29, italics added).

According to John's gospel, Jesus accused his opponents of not desiring this God-bestowed praise. "How can you believe," he asked, "when you receive glory from one another and do not seek *the glory that comes from the only God?*" (John 5:44, italics added).

Perhaps the clearest reference in the New Testament to what Lewis called "the weight of glory" is found in 1 Peter, Todd said. There we read that "the tested genuineness of your faith—more precious [to God] than gold that perishes though it is tested by fire—[will] be found to result in praise and glory and honor at the revelation of Jesus Christ" (1:7).

In "The Weight of Glory," Lewis emphasizes how staggering these texts are. It seems incredible, mind-blowing, almost farfetched that God would lavish us with glory, that the Bible not only highlights the creation-to-Creator, humanity-to-God direction of praise but also highlights its Creator-to-creation, its God-to-humanity direction. "How does this work?" I wondered out loud in Todd's flat. "How can *God* glorify *us?*"

Clustered around the New Testament affirmations of future praise and honor for Christians are other affirmations that go a long way toward answering my question, as I've come to see. In the first place, the New Testament affirms the forgiveness of sins and our "inclusion" or "incorporation" in Christ as the basis for our receiving glory from God. According to Paul, for example, Christians are able to stand "holy and blameless" before God because "we have redemption through [Christ's] blood, the forgiveness of our trespasses" (Ephesians 1:4, 7). God will judge the secrets of men, Paul says similarly in Romans, *according to the gospel* and *by Christ Jesus,* the one who died to make forgiveness a reality (2:16; 3:21–26). The divine accolade redounding to our glory on the judgment day will be based on our forgiveness and justification.

142

But not only on our forgiveness. Christians' glory will be in accord with the transforming work of God's Spirit in our lives. When Jesus died and rose from the dead, he unleashed power to live in a way that pleases God, a way that will elicit God's praise. "Being therefore exalted at the right hand of God, and having received from the Father the promise of the Holy Spirit, [-Jesus] has poured out this that you yourselves are seeing and hearing," Peter said in a sermon to the crowd who witnessed firsthand the Pentecost display of the Spirit's power in Jerusalem (Acts 2:33). According to Paul, on this side of Pentecost, we live our daily lives by the Spirit. "For through the Spirit, by faith, we ourselves eagerly wait for the hope of righteousness"—the hope of future glory (Galatians 5:5). Praise from God, as Lewis recognized, is only possible because of the work of Christ and his Spirit.

***

But Lewis doesn't end there. Pondering this future glory, he says, has implications for how we think about our lives now. God's acceptance of us in the future, his being pleased with us, means that we may be pleased with ourselves in the here and now as we live our daily Christian lives; or, more precisely, we may be pleased that we are pleasing to God.

In Lewis's view, however, this isn't the same thing as pride. "There will be no room for vanity ... when the redeemed soul, beyond all hope and nearly beyond belief, learns at last that she has pleased him whom she was created to please."[8]

At that moment,

she will be free from the miserable illusion that it is her own doing. With no taint of what we should now call self-approval she will most innocently rejoice in the thing that God has made her to be, and the moment which heals her old inferiority complex forever will also drown her pride deeper than Prospero's book. Perfect humility dispenses with modesty. If God is satisfied with the work, the work may be satisfied with itself.[9]

According to Lewis, the promise of a future accolade from God means we can be satisfied with our work—our lives, our imperfect efforts to serve and love God—now.

Many Christians, however, even many great and mature ones, saints and careful theologians throughout church history, have questioned this idea of Lewis's. These Christians have thought that the closer we get to God, the more we must sense our own remaining corruption and sinfulness. The ladder of spiritual growth is one of paradox: the higher we climb toward heaven, the lower we see ourselves sinking into the muck and mire of our shortcomings. "Oh ... if God's people knew me, as God knows, they would not think so highly of my zeal and resolution for God, as perhaps now they do!" exclaimed the melancholy American missionary David Brainerd. "I could not but desire they should see how heartless and irresolute I was, that they might be undeceived, and 'not think of me above what they ought to think.'"[10] In a similar vein, the Russian Orthodox Christian and novelist Leo Tolstoy rued his inability to live up to God's standards. "I do not preach," he wrote in self-disgust to critics who were all too aware of his moral failures. "I am not able to preach, although I passionately wish to. I can preach only through my actions, and my actions are vile.... I am guilty, and vile, and worthy of contempt for my failure to carry them out."[11] Brainerd and Tolstoy are just two examples. There have been and are still many Christians who express similar sentiments.

I know why these Christians talk this way. Listening to them, I hear echoes of my own feelings. As a Christian wrestling with homosexuality, I too, at times, feel like Tolstoy—"guilty, and vile, and worthy of contempt for my failure" to live out God's ideal. And yet, since reading C.S. Lewis's "The Weight of Glory," I wonder: Does the New Testament really support this kind of negative self-conception?

My landlord once decided to renovate the bathroom in my apartment while I was living there. Things had gotten a little drippy and dilapidated, and when he hired someone to help him rip up the curling linoleum and replace the shower and cabinets with new ones from Home Depot, I didn't complain. I remember coming back from a job interview one day and, as I walked past the open bathroom door, hearing the pounding of a hammer and the cracking of plastic. I poked my head inside to see what was happening. The bathtub was broken open like a giant eggshell, and a stench of moldy, water-damaged boards and soap scum was wafting out through the jagged fissures. As I thought about it later, I realized that this image is the one many people have of their Christian lives—on the outside, clean and shiny, but on the inside, beneath the cracks, full of the moral equivalent of loathsome smells and mildew. But is this really the Christian vision? Is my stinky bathroom really the right metaphor for our new life in Christ—the more you look under the surface, the more dirt you find?

It is true that Paul viewed his efforts at obedience even as a Christian to be flawed and tainted by sin. Like a glass of water with a drop of ink dissolved in it, everything we are and do, even as "new creatures," is tinged by our fallenness.[12] "We all stumble in many ways," states James epigrammatically (3:2). And John warns: "If we say we have no sin, we deceive ourselves, and the truth is not in us" (1 John 1:8). Yet, for all this, it would seem that the whole tenor of the New Testament is strikingly positive when it comes to describing the Christian experience of trying to live in a way that pleases God. Not triumphalistic, but positive. Maybe even *optimistic.* In short, rotten fruit isn't the right analogy.[13]

Sounding forth like a trumpet from the pages of the New Testament gospels, letters, poems, and visions is a message that something dramatic, invasive—something apocalyptic—happened in the death and resurrection of Jesus and the sending of the Holy Spirit. The world was irrevocably changed by the events of Good Friday, Easter Sunday, and Pentecost. By the same token, the New Testament declares that something liberating, transforming, and renewing happens every time a person turns to Jesus. Through faith in the Son, a believer's "heart," the core of her being, is "cleansed" and indwelt by the Spirit (Acts 15:8–9; John 14:16–17). From the inside out, from top to bottom, a believer is "sanctified," set apart by God's special favor (1 Corinthians 1:2; Ephesians 1:4; Hebrews 10:10); called out and rescued from the domain of darkness and transferred to the kingdom of the Son and his "marvelous light" (Colossians 1:13; 1 Peter 2:9–10); enabled to keep the requirements of God's law (Romans 8:3; 13:8–10); filled with the fruit of righteousness, the fruit produced by the Spirit (Galatians 5:22–23; Philippians 1:11). Through faith, a believer possesses God's own seed and an abiding "anointing" from God (1 John 2:27; 3:9); she is taught by God himself to love her fellow brothers and sisters in Christ (1 Thes-salo-nians 4:9). "Thanks be to God," exclaimed Paul to the Romans, "that you who were once slaves of sin have become obedient from the heart..., and having been set free from sin, have become slaves of righteousness" (6:17–18).

The human heart that has been redeemed by Christ has been made new. And that heart leads to a new way of life. And that way of life will be honored when Jesus appears on the last day with a "weight of glory," a divine accolade.

What might this mean for a homosexual Christian?

***

More and more, I have the sense that what many of us need is a new conception of our perseverance in faith. We need to reimagine ourselves and our struggles. The temptation for me is to look at my bent and broken sexuality and conclude that, with it, I will never be able to please God, to walk in a manner worthy of his calling, to hear his praise. But what if I had a conception of God-glorifying faith, holiness, and righteousness that included within it a profound element of struggle and stumbling? What if I were to view my homosexual orientation, temptations, and occasional failures not as damning disqualifications for living a Christian life but rather as part and parcel of what it means to live by faith in a world that is fallen and scarred by sin and death?

-"People with same-sex attractions who profess Christian faith ... will accept their homosexual desires as their cross—as a providential part of their struggle to glorify God and save their lives in a sinful world," writes Thomas Hopko, an Eastern Orthodox priest. He adds:

> They will view their same-sex attractions as a crucial part of their God-given path to sancti-ty..., both for themselves and potential sexual

partners. And they will see their refusal to act out their feelings sexually as an extraordinary opportunity for imitating Christ and participating in his saving Passion. They will, in a word, take up their erotic sexual desires, with their desire to love and be loved, as an essential part of their personal striving to fulfill St. Paul's appeal: "I beseech you therefore, brethren, by the mercies of God, that you present your bodies a living sacrifice, holy, acceptable to God, which is your reasonable service."[14]

My homosexuality, my exclusive attraction to other men, my grief over it and my repentance, my halting effort to live fittingly in the grace of Christ and the power of the Spirit—gradually I am learning not to view all of these things as confirmations of my rank corruption and hypocrisy. I am instead, slowly but surely, learning to view that journey—of struggle, failure, repentance, restoration, renewal in joy, and persevering, agonized obedience—as what it looks like for the Holy Spirit to be transforming me on the basis of Christ's cross and his Easter morning triumph over death.

The Bible calls the Christian struggle against sin *faith* (Hebrews 12:3–4; 10:37–39). It calls the Christian fight against impure cravings *holiness* (Romans 6:12–13, 22). So I am trying to appropriate these biblical descriptions for myself. I am learning to look at my daily wrestling with disordered desires and call it *trust.* I am learning to look at my battle to keep from giving in to my temptations and call it *sanctification.* I am learning to see that my flawed, imperfect, yet never-giving-up faithfulness is precisely the spiritual fruit that God will praise me for on the last day, to the ultimate honor of Jesus Christ.

My continuing struggle for holiness as a gay Christian can be a fragrant aroma to the Father. I am coming to believe that it will be, in C.S. Lewis's words, "an ingredient in the divine happiness."

***

The gospel tells us that our obedience matters to God, that he takes note of it. He sees our struggle to live faithfully with same-sex attractions. He helps us with grace through his Son and Spirit. He values our perseverance.

In J.R.R. Tolkien's The Lord of the Rings trilogy, there is a wonderful scene in which Sam, Frodo's companion on the quest to destroy the evil ring made by the dark lord Sauron, reflects on the "narrative quality" of his and Frodo's experience.

> We shouldn't be here at all [Sam says to Frodo], if we'd known more about it before we started. But I suppose it's often that way. The brave things in the old tales and songs, Mr. Frodo: adventures, as I used to call them. I used to think that they were things the wonderful folk of the stories went out and looked for, because they wanted them, because they were exciting and life

was a bit dull, a kind of sport, as you might say. But that's not the way of it with the tales that really mattered, or the ones that stay in the mind. Folk seem to have been just landed in them, usually—their paths were laid that way, as you put it. But I expect they had lots of chances, like us, of turning back, only they didn't. And if they had, we shouldn't know, because they'd have been forgotten. We hear about those as just went on—and not all to a good end, mind you; at least not to what folk inside a story and not outside it call a good end. You know, coming home, and finding things all right, though not quite the same—like old Mr. Bilbo. But those aren't always the best tales to hear, though they may be the best tales to get landed in! I wonder what sort of tale we've fallen into.[15]

Sam goes on to wonder if he and Frodo will someday be talked about, be remembered, by those who recount their story. In Peter Jackson's wonderful film version of *The Two Towers,* Sam says:

By rights we shouldn't even be here [on this quest]. But we are.... I wonder if people will ever say, "Let's hear about Frodo and the Ring." And they'll say, "Yes, that's one of my favorite stories. Frodo was really courageous, wasn't he, Dad." "Yes, my boy, the most famousest of hobbits. And that's saying a lot."

Many times in my experience with homosexuality I have wished my life was different, that I had some other burden to bear—anything but this one. But I have also felt that if Someone is watching—taking note; caring about each footfall, each bend in the trail; marking my progress—then the burden may be bearable.

When the road is long and the loneliness and sheer longing threaten to extinguish hope, it helps to remember that, like Frodo and Sam, I, too, am in a grand tale, with an all-seeing, all-caring Reader or Listener who also happens to be in some mysterious way the Author. Sam of The Lord of the Rings trilogy believed there would be listeners and readers who would want to know the story of this struggle. I believe that in my case, too, there is Someone who cares about my story. Unlike Sam and Frodo's, my story and the depths of my struggle may never be observed or known by any human watcher. But I can still endure—I can keep on fighting to live faithfully as a believer bearing my broken sexuality—so long as I have the assurance that my life matters to God, that, wonder of all wonders, my faith pleases him, that somehow it makes him smile.

***

Martin Hallett is a celibate homosexual Christian who grasped many of the insights I have been writing about in this chapter long before I did. He is farther down the road than I am, and I look to him as a scout who has run ahead and reported back to those of us who are tempted to lag behind.

Martin holds to the traditional Christian teaching about homosexual activity. Like me and many other gay believers, he is convinced that God's will for him is to abstain from homoerotic behavior. Yet, perhaps surprisingly, Martin speaks of his homosexual orientation as a "gift." So many people, he says, can only see their experiences of homosexuality "as problems to be 'defeated,' and 'handicaps' to be 'healed.'"[16] But for Martin, his homosexuality is a "positive thing"—not so much because it is good in and of itself but rather because, under God's sovereignty, it can lead to blessings. "Scripture continually shows us that even bad things can have value," Martin says frequently.[17]

Early on in his life as a Christian living in England, Martin found that his homosexuality gave him a ministry in the church. Under the guidance of a wise vicar, Canon Roy Barker, Martin shared his story through an organized event for anyone in the church interested in the topic of homosexuality. "[Canon Barker] saw a lot of potential in me," Martin would later write, "—not despite my homosexuality, but because of it."[18] Martin says that, though he couldn't see it at the time, these early ministry experiences caused him to see his homosexual orientation as valuable, as positive, as something that could be used to help others in the body of Christ.

"My life story..., 'written' by God, who is sovereign, include[s] my sexuality, which is a gift to the church," writes Martin. "I am very grateful that I see this experienced nearly every day of my life. I am able to see my struggles and failures, as well as my victories, as being of value to others."[19] Our sexuality "can be a gift to others," he continues. "We may use it to encourage someone else. We may use it simply to love and trust another person with a sexual confession."

Martin compares this process of entrusting another person with the story of our homosexuality to "unwrapping a gift." "The gift is one of self-disclosure. You are trusting the other with personal information that can often cost a lot, but it is a wonderful act of love."[20] I think of my own experiences of opening up the narrative of my journey as a homosexual Christian with friends at my church in Minneapolis. Invariably (though I didn't believe them at the time) they told me it felt like love; my trusting them enough to share my story was an honor, they said, a sacred trust. "We need to recognize the ministry that we and others have, not despite our unique stories and situation, but because of them," says Martin.[21]

Not only does our homosexuality give us a unique ministry within the church; it provides us with a greater sense of our woundedness and therefore of our dependence on God. It forces us, day by day, to rely not so much on total moral transformation now but rather on our forgiveness, the erasure of our guilt through Christ's death on the cross. Our homosexuality, says Martin, "draws us closer to God."[22]

Near the beginning of his Christian life, Martin went through a time of freedom from oppressive sexual temptation. He happily served in his large evangelical church and was blessed with a thriving ministry to many different people. Later, though, temptation returned. Martin had been involved in same-sex partnerships before he came to Christ, and now the old desires and struggles were reemerging. But it was too late to go back. Martin knew he had come too far to return. "I wanted to go on with Christ," he says, "and I began to see even my struggles as positive. Through them, my sexuality was telling me more about myself, and ultimately more about God's love and forgiveness."[23]

For Martin, homosexuality "speaks" of brokenness, of past hurts and wounds.[24] It calls us to consider our own lives and to trust in the mystery of God's providence and his gift of redemption through Christ. With patience and openness to the good that may come even from evil, we can learn to "hear" the voice of our sexuality, to listen to its call. We can learn to "appreciate the value of our story and the stories of others, because God is the 'potter' or 'storyteller'."[25]

Slowly, ever so slowly, I am learning to do this. I am learning that my struggle to live faithfully before God in Christ with my homosexual orientation is pleasing to him. And I am waiting for the day when I will receive the divine accolade, when my labor of trust and hope and self-denial will be crowned with his praise. "Well done, good and faithful servant," the Lord Christ will say. "Enter into the joy of your master."

AFTERWORD BY KATHRYN GREENE-MCCREIGHT

If one member suffers, all suffer together...

1 Corinthians 12:26

In 1 Corinthians 12, the apostle Paul speaks about the unity of the body of Christ. He notes that each part of the body has a unique role and function. "The eye cannot say to the hand, 'I have no need of you....'" (1 Corinthians 12:21). All who claim Christ as risen Lord are members of his body and are individually members of it.

In the late 1960s and early 1970s, the Western world witnessed the development of various movements of liberation, among them gay liberation. Since that time, we have seen the increasing cultural acceptance of gay and lesbian people on their own terms. This movement has made inroads, not only into Western society, but also into Christian churches of every denomination and communion, particularly in the United States.

Wesley Hill does not locate himself within the gay liberation movement as it has gained power within Christian churches. He displays for the reader his own life as a homosexual, with his desires and passions toward his own sex. This he shares with those in the gay liberation movement. But Wesley disagrees in his response to his passions. Since his highest love is the triune God, he understands his unique vocation (as a gay Christian) to be celibate.

In keeping with the apostolic teaching and tradition, Wesley Hill accepts that homosexual sex is not part of God's original creative intention for humanity. Rather, it is a tragic sign of human sin, which issues in fractured relationships. His thesis will no doubt be unpopular on both the left and the right of this polarized debate. Even so, he can say: "To renounce homosexual behavior is to say yes to full, rich, abundant life" (see page 79). Jesus' promise is true for the homosexual as well: "I have come that they may life and have it abundantly" (John 10:10).

Wesley Hill's experience poses a crucial question to Christian churches on both the left and right of the debate over homosexual sex. As a gay man, he is more than willing to sacrifice a life of partnership with another gay man because of his lived-out obedience to the triune God. However, loneliness remains a fact of his life. This is a reality faced not only by those who choose a celibate gay life but by any unmarried Christian.

How can this stark loneliness exist in the life of a member of the body of Christ? *If one member suffers, all suffer together.* For the heterosexual Christian, the loneliness of one can possibly become the companionship of two, but for the gay/lesbian celibate Christian, the loneliness they face is potentially unremitting. The reality of loneliness and isolation of the celibate gay/lesbian Christian needs to be held close in thought and prayer.

In light of all this, how should we respond? Do we (heterosexual Christians) simply cast our glances aside from our brothers and sisters who struggle with homosexual desires? Can we continue to ignore the isolation these brothers and sisters experience within the body of Christ? Are we afraid to hear about the same-sex desire of brothers or sisters for whom Jesus Christ died, even when they choose the narrow path of celibacy, despite the attendant trials of loneliness and solitude. "The eye cannot say to the hand, 'I have no need of you,' nor again the head to the feet, 'I have no need of you.' ... If one member suffers, all suffer together; if one member is honored, all rejoice together. Now you are the body of Christ and individually members of it" (1 Corinthians 12:21, 26–27).

We who are the body of Christ must show the love, joy, hope, and fellowship of the gospel to all who are part of the body. This is especially true in this day and age with regard to those who, for the sake of the narrow gate of the gospel, find their vocation in celibacy—even when it may include personal pain and isolation.

160

NOTES

Introduction

[1] Philip Yancey, *Soul Survivor* (New York: Double-day, 2001), 269–70.

[2] See, for just a few examples among many recent articles and books, Stephen E. Fowl, *Engaging Scripture: A Model for Theological Interpretation* (Oxford: Blackwell, 1998); Jeffrey Heskins, *Face to Face: Gay and Lesbian Clergy on Holiness and Life Together* (Grand Rapids: Eerdmans, 2006); Sylvia C. Keesmaat, "Welcoming in the Gentiles: A Biblical Model for Decision Making," in *Living Together in the Church: Including Our Differences,* ed. Greig Dunn and Chris Ambidge (Toronto: Anglican Book Centre, 2004), 30–49.

[3] Chad W. Thompson, *Loving Homosexuals as Jesus Would: A Fresh Christian Approach* (Grand Rapids: Brazos, 2004).

[4] J.I. Packer, "Why I Walked," *Christianity Today* 47 (January 21, 2003): 46.

[5] Martin Hallett, "Homosexuality: Handicap and Gift," in *Holiness and Sexuality: Homosexuality in a Biblical Context,* ed. David Peterson (Carlisle, UK: Paternoster, 2004), 121.

[6] Ibid., 130–31, 145.

[7] C.S. Lewis, *The Weight of Glory and Other Addresses* (1949; repr., New York: HarperCollins, 2001), 39.

Prelude: Washed and Waiting

[1]   Barbara Brown Taylor, *When God Is Silent* (Cambridge, Mass.: Cowley, 1998), 110.

[2]   Gordon Hugenberger, "Questions and Answers on Issues Related to Homosexuality and Same-Sex Marriage," June 15, 2004, http://www.par kstreet.org/qa_homosexuality.

[3]   Richard Bewes, "The New Hampshire Decision: Statement from All Souls Church, Langham Place, London Wi, November 2003."

[4]   Henri J.M. Nouwen, *The Return of the Prodigal Son: A Story of Homecoming* (New York: Doubleday, 1992), 14.

[5]   Rainer Maria Rilke, *Letters to a Young Poet* (New York: Norton, 1954), 34.

Chapter 1: A Story-Shaped Life

[1]   See especially Richard B. Hays, *The Moral Vision of the New Testament* (San Francisco: HarperSanFrancisco, 1996), chapter 16, "Homosexuality." The church's traditional teaching on homosexuality is being challenged today by churches and individual Christians (for a carefully reasoned, elegant example of such a challenge, see Eugene Rogers, *Sexuality and the Christian Body: Their Way into the Triune God* [Oxford: Blackwell, 1999]), but Hays's chapter still represents the widespread consensus of the majority of churches because it takes seriously the plain sense of Scripture.

[2] Congregation for the Doctrine of the Faith, *Letter to the Bishops of the Catholic Church on the Pastoral Care of Homosexual Persons* (October 1986), paragraph 7, http://www.vatican.va/roman_curia/congregations/cfaith/documents/rc_con_cfaith_doc_19861001_homosexual-persons_en.html.

[3] John Piper, "Beliefs about Homosexual Behavior and Ministering to Homosexual Persons: Resolution Passed by the Baptist General Conference in Annual Meeting, Estes Park, Colorado" (June 27, 1992), http://www.desiringgod.org/ResourceLibrary/Articles/ByDate/1992/1499_Beliefs_about_Homosexual_Behavior_and_Ministering_to_Homosexual_Persons/.

[4] George A. Lindbeck, *The Nature of Doctrine: Religion and Theology in a Postliberal Age* (Philadelphia: Westminster, 1984), 34.

[5] Ibid., 35.

[6] Scott Bader-Saye, "Living the Gospels: Morality and Politics," in *The Cambridge Companion to the Gospels,* ed. Stephen C. Barton (Cambridge: Cambridge University Press, 2006), 282 n. 14.

[7] Hays, *Moral Vision of the New Testament,* 393.

[8] Robert Jenson, "Dr. Jenson on what makes for a good bishop" (a letter written to the Right Reverend Stephen Bouman), http://www.freerepublic.com/focus/f-religion/1857394/posts.

[9] John Webster, "The Church as Witnessing Community," *Scottish Bulletin of Evangelical Theology* 21 (2003): 22.

[10] Frederick Buechner, *Wishful Thinking: A Seeker's ABC* (1973; repr., San Francisco: HarperSanFrancisco, 1993), 65.

[11] Quoted in Hays, *Moral Vision of the New Testament,* 401.

[12] Andrew F. Walls, *The Missionary Movement in Christian History* (Maryknoll, N.Y.: Orbis, 1996), 8.

[13] Hays, *Moral Vision of the New Testament,* 391–92.

[14] Stephen Neill, *A History of Christian Missions* (New York: Penguin, 1990), 86.

[15] Quoted in Henri J.M. Nouwen, *Reaching Out: The Three Movements of the Spiritual Life* (Garden City, N.Y.: Doubleday, 1975), 24.

[16] Quoted in Lane Dennis, ed., *The Letters of Francis A. Schaeffer* (Westchester, Ill.: Crossway, 1985), 195.

[17] Philip Yancey, *The Jesus I Never Knew* (Grand Rapids: Zondervan, 1995), 274.

[18] Wendell Berry, *Jayber Crow: The Life Story of Jayber Crow, Barber, of the Port William Membership, as Written by Himself* (New York: Counterpoint, 2000).

[19] Ibid., 10.

[20] Ibid. 248.

[21] Ibid., 247.

[22] C.S. Lewis, *Mere Christianity* (1943; repr., New York: HarperCollins, 2001), 142.

[23] Karl Barth, *Church Dogmatics* III/2 (Edinburgh: T&T Clark, 1960), 43, italics added.

[24] Walter Moberly, "The Use of Scripture in Contemporary Debate about Homosexuality," *Theology* 103 (2000): 254.

[25] Ibid., 258.

Interlude: The Beautiful Incision

[1] Henri J.M. Nouwen, *The Return of the Prodigal Son: A Story of Homecoming* (New York: Doubleday, 1992).

[2] Ibid., 69–70, 71–72.

[3] Michael Ford, *Wounded Prophet: A Portrait of Henri J.M. Nouwen* (New York: Doubleday, 2002), 157.

[4] Ibid., 159; cf. Philip Yancey, *Soul Survivor: How My Faith Survived the Church* (New York: Doubleday, 2001), 314.

[5] Henri J.M. Nouwen, *Adam: God's Beloved* (London: Darton, Longman and Todd, 1997), 38.

[6] Yancey, *Soul Survivor,* 315.

[7] Michael O'Laughlin, *Henri Nouwen: His Life and Vision* (Maryknoll, N.Y.: Orbis, 2005), 85.

[8] Quoted in ibid.

[9] Nouwen, *Return of the Prodigal Son,* 73.

[10] See O'Laughlin, *Henri Nouwen,* 85.

[11] Yancey, *Soul Survivor,* 301.

[12] Ford, *Wounded Prophet,* 170.

[13]   Yancey, *Soul Survivor,* 302, order slightly altered.

[14]   Ford, *Wounded Prophet,* 73, 92.

[15]   Ibid., 140.

[16]   Ibid., 142, 143.

[17]   Ibid., 73.

[18]   Henri Nouwen, *The Wounded Healer* (New York: Random House, 1979), 84.

Chapter 2: The End of Loneliness

[1]   Rowan Williams, "The Body's Grace," in *Theology and Sexuality: Classic and Contemporary Readings,* ed. Eugene F. Rogers Jr. (Oxford: Blackwell, 2002), 313.

[2]   Wendell Berry, *Hannah Coulter: A Novel* (Washington, D.C.: Shoemaker & Hoard, 2004), 71.

[3]   Ibid., 109.

[4]   Ibid., 65.

[5]   Denis Haack, movie review of *Garden State,* http://www.ransomfellowship.org/articledetail.asp?AID=114&B=Denis%20Haack&TID=2.

[6]   For more on the idea of intentional Christian community, see, e.g., Jonathan Wilson-Hargrove, *New Monasticism: What It Has to Say to Today's Church* (Grand Rapids: Brazos, 2008). For the church's historic views on celibacy and sexual abstinence, see Peter Brown, *The Body and Society: Men, Women, and Sexual Renunciation in Early Christianity* (20th anniv. ed.; New York: Columbia University

Press, 2008). Perhaps this is the best place to mention that many homosexual Christians are likely to find themselves often falling short of these various "options" for Christian faithfulness. In my view, the church should continue to explain the biblical and theological reasons for avoiding same-sex erotic activity and help homosexual Christians live up to that ideal but also continually, repeatedly show grace and understanding toward those who fail.

[7]   "A Personal Journey," the testimony of a gay evangelical Christian, http://www.courage.org.uk/articles/article.asp?id=145.

[8]   Quoted in Misty Irons, "'Immoral' and 'Faggot,'" March 19, 2007 (blog post), http://moremusingson.blogspot.com/2007/03/immoral-and-faggot.html.

[9]   Williams, "Body's Grace," 311–12.

[10]   J. Louis Martyn, *Galatians: A New Translation with Introduction and Commentary* (Anchor Bible 33A; New York: Doubleday, 1997), 381.

[11]   Henri J.M. Nouwen, *Sabbatical Journey: A Diary of His Final Year* (New York: Crossroad, 1998), 25.

[12]   Quoted in Agnieszka Tennant, "A Shrink Gets Stretched," *Christianity Today,* May 2003, http://www.christianitytoday.com/ct/2003/may/7.52.html.

[13] Richard B. Hays, *The Moral Vision of the New Testament* (San Francisco: Harper-SanFrancisco, 1996), 402.

[14] Hafiz, "My Eyes So Soft," in *The Gift: Poems by Hafiz,* trans. Daniel Ladinsky (New York: Penguin, 1999), 277. Copyright © 1999 by Daniel Ladinsky. Used by permission of Daniel Ladinsky.

[15] C.S. Lewis, *The Weight of Glory and Other Addresses* (1949; repr., New York: Harper-Collins, 2001), 41–42.

[16] Oliver O'Donovan, *Resurrection and Moral Order: An Outline for Evangelical Ethics* (Grand Rapids: Eerdmans, 1986), 70.

Postlude: "Thou Art Lightning and Love"

[1] Frederick Buechner, *Speak What We Feel, Not What We Ought to Say: Reflections on Literature and Faith* (San Francisco: HarperSanFrancisco, 2004), 24. For the biographical information that follows, I am indebted to Buechner's book, as well as Robert Bernard Martin, *Gerard Manley Hopkins: A Very Private Life* (New York: G.P. Putnam's Sons, 1991).

[2] Buechner, *Speak What We Feel,* 23.

[3] Quoted in ibid., 24.

[4] Ibid.

[5] Gerard Manley Hopkins, "I Wake and Feel"; all poems hereafter are cited by title and are

taken from Gerard Manley Hopkins, *Hopkins: Poems and Prose* (New York: Knopf, 1995).

[6]   "God's Grandeur."

[7]   "Spring and Fall: To a Young Child."

[8]   "I Wake and Feel."

[9]   "No Worst."

[10] "No Worst."

[11] "To Seem the Stranger."

[12] Buechner, *Speak What We Feel*, 23.

[13] "The Wreck of the Deutschland," stanza 9.

[14] "Carrion Comfort."

[15] "In the Valley of the Elwy."

[16] "The Lantern Out of Doors."

[17] "That Nature Is a Heraclitean Fire and of the Comfort of the Resurrection."

Chapter 3: The Divine Accolade

[1]   Michael O'Laughlin, *Henri Nouwen: His Life and Vision* (Maryknoll, N.Y.: Orbis, 2005), 85.

[2]   Dallas Willard, *The Divine Conspiracy: Rediscovering Our Hidden Life in God* (San Francisco: HarperSanFrancisco, 1997), 165.

[3]   Ibid., 164.

[4]   Robert W. Jenson, *Systematic Theology*, 2 vols. (Oxford: Oxford University Press, 1999), 2:141.

[5]   For amplification of many of the points in this chapter, see Todd A. Wilson, *Praise from God: The Promise of Glory at the Judgment Seat of Christ* (forthcoming).

[6]   C.S. Lewis, *The Weight of Glory and Other Addresses* (1949; repr., New York: Harper-Collins, 2001), 34, 36.

[7]   Ibid., 38–39.

[8]   Ibid., 37, order slightly altered.

[9]   Ibid., 37–38.

[10] Jonathan Edwards, ed., *The Life and Diary of David Brainerd* (Grand Rapids: Baker, 1989), 372. My thanks to Todd Wilson for drawing my attention to this reference and many others like it in Brainerd's journals.

[11] Quoted in Philip Yancey, *Soul Survivor: How My Faith Survived the Church* (New York: Doubleday, 2001), 130.

[12] See Miroslav Volf, *Free of Charge: Giving and Forgiving in a Culture Stripped of Grace* (Grand Rapids: Zondervan, 2005), 98, for this analogy. The passage is worth quoting in full, since Volf makes the same point I am trying to make here: "Even if all of us are sinners from head to toe, none of us is a sinner through and through, with nothing good remaining in us. As sinners, we are still God's good creatures. To illustrate the relationship between being a good creature and being a sinner, Reformation theologians used the analogy of water and ink. Water is the good creation, ink is sin, and the sinner is a glass of water with a few drops of ink. All the water in the glass is tainted,

but it's still mostly water, not ink. Analogously, all our good deeds are marred by sin, but they are still mostly good deeds, not crimes masquerading as merits."

[13]   In 1 Corinthians 15:9, Paul writes: "I am the least of the apostles, unworthy to be called an apostle, because I persecuted the church of God" (cf. 1 Timothy 1:13, 15: "Formerly I was a blasphemer, persecutor, and insolent opponent.... Christ Jesus came into the world to save sinners, of whom I am the foremost"). This has led many people to think that Paul had a self-conception similar to that of Brainerd and Tolstoy. However, these texts probably refer to Paul's *former* manner of life in Judaism, when he violently sought to destroy the nascent faith in Jesus. After his experience with the risen Christ on the Damascus road (see Acts 9:1–19), when he realized his ignorance and error, he became an apostle of Christ and seemed to have a "robust conscience" as a Christian believer from then on, untroubled by guilt feelings or an overwhelming sense of being corrupt and constantly displeasing to God in his thoughts and actions. "I do not even judge myself. I am not aware of anything against myself," he writes (1 Corinthians 4:3–4). Passages like this could be multiplied. For a helpful statement of this view of Paul, drawing on many different texts, see Gordon

Fee, *God's Empowering Presence: The Holy Spirit in the Letters of Paul* (Peabody, Mass.: Hendrickson, 1994), 420–71, 508–15, 816–22.

When Paul writes in Romans 7, "I am of the flesh, sold under sin" and "I do not do what I want, but I do the very thing I hate" and "The evil I do not want is what I keep on doing" (vv. 14, 15, 19), he is probably not referring to sinful actions he commits as a Christian. Rather, with these statements Paul seems to be narrating the corporate experience of the people of Israel, their experience of idolatry and disobedience that eventually led to their exile in Assyria and Babylon as recorded in the Old Testament, as well as the present-day experience of those "under the law." In Romans 6 and 8, he expresses a sharply contrasting view of himself and other Christians in the new era of the Spirit: "Thanks be to God, that you who were once slaves of sin have become obedient from the heart ... and, having been set free from sin, have become slaves of righteousness" (6:17–18). "The righteous requirement of the law [is] fulfilled in us" (8:4). "You ... are not in the flesh but in the Spirit" (8:9). For engaging commentaries that support this reading of Romans 6–8, see especially Douglas J. Moo, *Romans,* The NIV Application Commentary (Grand Rapids: Zondervan, 2000); Tom Wright, *Paul for Everyone: Romans: Chapters 1–8* (Louisville: Westminster John Knox, 2004); and Anthony A. Hoekema, *The*

Christian Looks at Himself (Grand Rapids: Eerdmans, 1975).

[14] Thomas Hopko, *Christian Faith and Same-Sex Attraction: Eastern Orthodox Reflections* (Ben Lomond, Calif.: Conciliar, 2006), 48. The passage from Paul that Hopko quotes is Romans 12:1.

[15] J.R.R. Tolkien, *The Two Towers,* part 2, The Lord of the Rings (repr., New York: Ballantine, 1965), 362. See also Ralph C. Wood, "Frodo's Faith, Middleearth Truths," *Christian Century* 120 (September 6, 2003): 20–25.

[16] Martin Hallett, "Homosexuality: Handicap and Gift," in *Holiness and Sexuality: Homosexuality in a Biblical Context,* ed. David Peterson (Carlisle, UK: Paternoster, 2004), 121.

[17] Ibid., 122; cf. 131.

[18] Ibid., 123.

[19] Ibid., 144.

[20] Ibid., 140.

[21] Ibid., 143.

[22] Ibid., 122.

[23] Ibid., 124.

[24] Ibid., 139.

[25] Ibid., 143.

Front Cover Flap

WASHED AND WAITING

How do the gospel, holiness, and indwelling sin play out in the life of a Christian struggling with same-sex attraction? And how do brothers and sisters in Christ show love to them? Wesley Hill offers wise counsel that is biblically faithful, theologically serious, and oriented to the life and practice of the church.

As a celibate gay Christian, Hill gives us a glimpse at what it looks like to wrestle first-hand with God's "No" to same-sex relationships. What does it mean for gay Christians to be faithful to God while struggling with the challenge of their homosexuality? What is God's will for believers who experience same-sex desires? Those who choose celibacy are often left to deal with loneliness and the hunger for relationships. How can gay Christians experience God's favor and blessing in the midst of a struggle that for many brings a crippling sense of shame and guilt?

Weaving together reflections from his own life and the lives of other Christians, such as Henri Nouwen and Gerard Manley Hopkins, Hill offers a fresh perspective on these questions. He advocates neither unqualified "healing" for those who struggle nor accommodation to temptation, but rather faithfulness in the midst of brokenness.

Back Cover Flap

WESLEY HILL graduated from Wheaton College and has an MA in Theology and Religion from Durham University, UK. He is currently working toward a PhD in New Testament at Durham and has written for *Books & Culture* and Ransom Fellowship's magazine, *Critique.*

Back Cover Material

IS THERE A PLACE FOR **CELIBATE, GAY CHRISTIANS** IN THE **CHURCH?**

Author Wesley Hill offers a theological memoir on temptation, loneliness, and the future hope of healing for gay men and women who want to be faithful to Christ.

"Any Christian who wants to grapple seriously, biblically, and charitably with our human sexuality needs to read this book."
ALAN JACOBS, professor, Wheaton College

"This is an incredibly, incredibly important book. It is a raw, insightful, honest, beautiful, guy-wrenching, gripping story that I pray many people will read."
DAN KIMBALL, author of They Like Jesus But Not the Church

"Straight people will gain an empathetic understanding of homosexuality, and gay and lesbian Christians committed to celibacy will find a companion who identifies with their pain and loneliness."
LISA GRAHAM McMINN, professor, George Fox University

Books For ALL Kinds of Readers

At ReadHowYouWant we understand that one size does not fit all types of readers. Our innovative, patent pending technology allows us to design new formats to make reading easier and more enjoyable for you. This helps improve your speed of reading and your comprehension. Our EasyRead printed books have been optimized to improve word recognition, ease eye tracking by adjusting word and line spacing as well as minimizing hyphenation. Our EasyRead SuperLarge editions have been developed to make reading easier and more accessible for vision-impaired readers. We offer Braille and DAISY formats of our books and all popular E-Book formats.

We are continually introducing new formats based upon research and reader preferences. Visit our web-site to see all of our formats and learn how you can Personalize our books for yourself or as gifts. Sign up to Become A RHYW Registered Reader.

www.readhowyouwant.com

Made in the USA
Monee, IL
04 December 2020

50773563R00116